The easiest way to learn Marathi or any other language is to hear it spoken. This book successfully creates an 'audio effect for quicker grasp and assimilation. Rules of grammar have been explained only where absolutely necessary. A direct conversational style, with the help of a minimal vocabulary, phrases and sentences, makes learning Marathi effortless and pleasurable.

Correct pronunciation is a difficult exercise, specially for tongues not accustomed to Devnagri script. Diacritical marks have been provided to indicate different sounds and accents. By repeated practice,with the help of the book, one can acquire a working knowledge of spoken and written Marathi—and then, if one prefers, pursue advanced study.

TEACH YOURSELF MARATHI

R.S. DESHPANDE
G.E. SALPEKAR

HIPPOCRENE BOOKS
New York

First Hippocrene Edition, 1991
Second printing, 2005

For information, address:

HIPPOCRENE BOOKS, INC.
171 Madison Avenue
New York, NY 10016
www.hippocrenebooks.com

ISBN 0-87052-620-0

Printed in the United States of America.

FOREWORD

We have planned and written this book with a view to encouraging the study of Marathi in the various States of India. It will enable a student to acquire a working knowledge of the language and make him familiar with its phonetics and grammar.

Marathi, the language of the State of Maharashtra, is derived from Sanskrit, with which it shares an important linguistic characteristic, namely, the Devnagari script. Thus, it becomes easily accessible to Hindi-speaking Indians.

Outside Maharashtra, Marathi is understood in the Union Territory of Goa and in cities like Baroda, Indore and Gwalior, which were the capitals of the erstwhile Maratha princely states.

It has a rich literature, both prose and poetry. In the 13th century, it produced its greatest poet, Sant Dnyaneshwar (1275-1296), whose *Dnyaneshwari*, a commentary in verse on the *Geeta*, is revered in every Marathi home. Modern Marathi is a very vibrant language, capable of expressing the most subtle shades of literary and scientific concepts.

During the reign of the Deccan Sultans, it absorbed a substantial number of Urdu words. In the past two hundred years, it has also incorporated into its corpus several English words. Its *avant garde* playwrights and novelists have been translated into Hindi and other Indian languages.

We hope this primer will encourage readers to undertake a more exhaustive study of Marathi.

R.S. Deshpande
G.S. Salpekar

CONTENTS

Part I—Grammar

Chapter			*Page*
1	Key to Pronunciation	...	9
2	Nouns	...	17
3	Verbs	...	24
4	Cases	...	45
5	Adjectives	...	60
6	Numbers	...	70

Part II—Language

Lesson			
1	Kitee Wajale ?	...	78
2	Pustakālaya	...	80
3	Māze Ghar	....	83
4	Rasta	...	86
5	Vidyālaya	...	89
6	Mumbaee	...	92
7	Māzā Vyavasāy	...	95

Lesson		*Page*
8	Nātee	... 98
9	Sahal	... 101
10	Lagna-samārambha	... 104
11	Ek Pravās	... 106
12	Mahārāshtra	... 108
13	Kharedee	 112
14	Mhaṇee	... 117
	Glossary	... 120

Part I —Grammar

CHAPTER 1

KEY TO PRONUNCIATION

Since Marathi is written in the Devnagari script, both its vowels and consonants are pronounced as they will be in Sanskrit or Hindi.

Phonetic Symbols

(i) The sign (–) over the vowel 'a' denotes its modified form, the long aa आ (ā).

For instance,

a is pronounced as in 'above', but

ā would be pronounced as in 'arc'.

(ii) The dot (.) under a consonant denotes its aspirated form.

For instance,

d is pronounced as in 'thou', but

ḍ would be pronounced as in 'dance'.

Vowels

There are *twelve* vowels in Marathi :

अ = a as in above

आ = ā as in arc

इ = i as in it

ई = ee as in eel

उ = u as in bull

ऊ = oo as in moon

ए अे = e as in egg

ऐ अै = ei as in either

ओ = o as in oath

औ = ow as in how

अं = um as in umber

अः = ah as in aha !

—: o :—

Consonants

There are *thirty* consonants in Marathi :

क	=	ka; cu	as	in	cut
ख	=	kha	as	in	khaki
ग	=	ga	as	in	game
घ	=	gha	as	in	ghetto
च	=	cha	as	in	chain
छ	=	chha	as	in	Mlechha
ज	=	ja	as	in	jam
झ	=	jha	as	in	zero
ट	=	ṭa	as	in	target
ठ	=	ṭha	as	in	thakur
ड	=	ḍa	as	in	dance
ढ	=	ḍha	as	in	Dhaka (Dacca, Bangladesh)
ण	=	ng	as	in	spring
त	=	ta	as	in	tamasha

थ	=	tha	as	in	thanks
द	=	da	as	in	thou
ध	=	dha	as	in	dhotee
न	=	na	as	in	noun
प	=	pa	as	in	pair
फ	=	pha	as	in	fan
ब	=	ba	as	in	ball
भ	=	bha	as	in	bhaskar
म	=	ma	as	in	mango
य	=	ya	as	in	yesterday
र	=	ra	as	in	rain
ल	=	la	as	in	lamb
व	=	va	as	in	will
श,ष	=	sha	as	in	shall
स	=	sa	as	in	Sunday
ह	=	ha; hu	as	in	hut

—: o :—

A Consonant combining with a Vowel

There are *ten* different ways in which a consonant, *ka* for instance, can combine with a vowel.

These are

Vowel	*Vowel Sign*	*Combination*	*Combination Pronounced as in*
अ	अ has no vowel sign	क+अ=क	cup
आ	ा	क+आ=का	car
इ	ि	क+इ=कि	kit
ई	ी	क+ई=की	keep
उ	ु	क+उ=कु	kulak
ऊ	ू	क+ऊ=कू	cool
अे	े	क+अे=के	cane
अै	ै	क+अै=कै	kaiser
ओ	ो	क+ओ=को	coat
औ	ौ	क+औ=कौ	count
अं	ं	क+अं=कं	cumbersome

Thus, we have the following sequence of the consonant क (ka) :

क	का	कि	की
ka	kā	ki	kee
कु	कू	के	कै
ku	koo	ke	kei
को	कौ	कं	कः
ko	kow	kum	kah

All other consonants, i.e. from ख (kha) to ह (ha) follow the same sequence as in क (ka). Thus for (ख) kha, we get the following *ten* vowel combinations :

खा	खि	खी	खु	खू
khā	khi	khee	khu	khoo
खे	खै	खो	खौ	खं
khe	khei	kho	khow	khum

Note : (i) The consonant *kha* is written as a combination of *ra* (र) and *va* (व) : ख.

(ii) Both *ru* and *roo* are written as रु.

—: o —

A Consonant combining with another Consonant

(i) A consonant may combine with itself in which case it is first written incompletely, and the 'truncated' form is then joined to the full form of the consonant. Thus we have :

न्न, ण्ण, प्प, म्म, स्स, क्क, ज्ज, त्त (त्त) ;

ट्ट, ठ्ठ, ड्ड, ढ्ढ.

The latter may be written as :

ट्ट, ठ्ठ, ड्ड and ढ्ढ.

(ii) A consonant may combine with a different consonant. In this case too, the aforementioned rule is applicable to its written form. Thus, we have :

क+स=क्स	pronounced as in	politics, fix
क+व=क्व	,, ,,	quality, qualify
स+व=स्व	,, ,,	swan
त+व=त्व	,, ,,	twang*
प+ल=प्ल	,, ,,	plan
म+ब=म्ब	,, ,,	emblem
क+त=क्त	,, ,,	act*
व+ह=व्ह	,, ,,	whale, vale
क+ल=क्ल	,, ,,	clear
ब+ल=ब्ल	,, ,,	blood
क+ष=क्ष	,, ,,	Kurukshetra

[**t* pronounced soft]

(iii) The vowel र(ra) can be joined to another consonant in the following *six* different ways :

1. कर्म karma (fate)
   (*ra* preceding *ma* as in arm)

2. क्रम krama (sequence)
   (*ra* following *ka* as in crumb)

3. कृपा krupā (favour)
   (*ra* following *ka* as in cruel)

4. रात्र rātra (night)
   (*ra* following *ta* as in trial*)

5. राष्ट्र rāshtra (nation)
   (*ra* following both *sha* and *ṭa* as in strange pronounced shtrange)

6. प्रकाश prakāsh (light)
   (*ra* following *pa* as in practice).

[**t* pronounced soft]

—: o :—

CHAPTER 2

NOUNS
(Nāma)

There are *three* genders in Marāthi :

Pullinga (*masculine*) ;

Streelinga (*feminine*) ; and

Napusakalinga (*neuter*)

Genders are mainly based on sex, when the nouns stand for animate objects and on usage when they describe inanimate objects. However, in view of a large number of exceptions, it is virtually impossible to lay down precise rules, which would unfailingly help students to identify the genders of Marāthi nouns. Nevertheless, some broad guidelines may be mentioned. For instance :

(i) The following nouns, ending in the vowel ā (आ) are all masculine :

कारखाना (kārkhānā) factory

वारा (wārā) wind

नकाशा (nakāshā) map

खजिना (khajinā) treasure

खिसा (khisā) pocket

गालिचा (gālichā) carpet

आरसा (ārasā) mirror

खड्डा (khaḍ-ḍā) pit

फायदा (phaidā) profit

Exceptions : हवा(hawā) air; भाषा(bhāshā) language; कन्या (kanyā) daughter are feminine.

(ii) The following nouns ending in the vowel u (उ) are masculine :

पेरु (peru) guava

पशु (pashu) beast

(iii) The following nouns ending in a consonant are masculine :

सिंह (sinh) lion

वाघ (wāgh) tiger

कापूस (kāpoos) cotton

दगड (dagaḍ) stone

बैल (beil) bull

मित्र (mitra) friend

पोपट (popaṭ) parrot

(iv) The following nouns, though ending in a consonant, are feminine :

भिंत (bhinta) wall

दौत (dowt) inkpot

जखम (jakhama) wound

आग (āg) fire

वात (wāt) wick

(v) The following nouns ending in ई (ee) are feminine. This is the general rule.

माती (mātee) soil

खिडकी (khidkee) window

खोली (kholee) room

किल्ली (killee) key

खुर्ची (khurchee) chair

कादंबरी (kādambaree) novel

टोपी (ṭopee) cap

चौकशी (chowkashee) enquiry

Exceptions : पक्षी (pakshee) male bird

हत्ती (hattee) male elephant

धोबी (dhobee) male washerman
are masculine.

(vi) Inanimate objects are mostly neuter :

घर (ghar) house

कापड (kāpaḍ) cloth

दूध (doodh) milk

फूल (phool) flower

झाड (jhāḍ) tree.

Exceptions : तार (tār) wire, नाव (nāv) boat are feminine.

(vii) The following nouns, based on sex, are obviously masculine :

मुलगा (mulagā) boy

घोड़ा (ghoḍā) horse

राजा (rājā) king

नवरा (navarā) husband

पुरुष (purush) man

(viii) Similarly, the following nouns are obviously feminine :

स्त्री (stree) woman

बायको (bāyko) wife

मुलगी (mulagee) girl

राणी (rāṇee) queen

Change of Sex

If a masculine noun ends in आ (ā), its corresponding feminine form is obtained by changing आ into ई (ee). For example :

Mas.	*Fem.*
मुलगा (mulagā) boy	मुलगी (mulagee) girl
घोड़ा (ghoḍā) horse	घोड़ी (ghoḍee) mare
बकरा (bakarā) goat	बकरी (bakaree) she-goat
कुत्रा (kutrā) dog	कुत्री (kutree) bitch

Change of Number

(i) Masculine nouns ending in आ (ā) are converted into their plural form by changing आ into अे (e) For example :

Singular	*Plural*
मुलगा (mulaga)	मुलगे (mulage) boys
घोड़ा (ghoḍa)	घोड़े (ghoḍe) horses
राजा (rājā)	राजे (rāje) kings

(ii) Masculine nouns ending either in a vowel or a consonant do not change their form in the plural. Examples :

हत्ती (hattee) elephant; खांब (khāmb) pillar; पेरु (peru) guava; शत्रु (shatru) enemy; देव (dev) God.

(iii) Feminine nouns ending in a consonant are converted into their plurals by adding आ (ā) after the consonant. Examples:

Sing.	*Pl.*
तार (tār)	तारा (tārā) wires
नाव (nāv)	नावा (nāvā) boats

(iv) Feminine nouns ending in आ (ā) remain unchanged in the plural. Examples:

भाषा (bhāshā); कन्या (kanyā).

(v) Feminine nouns ending in ई (ee) are converted into their plurals by replacing ई (ee) with या (yā). Examples:

Sing.	*Pl.*
खिडकी (khiḍkee)	खिडक्या (khiḍkyā) windows
खोली (kholee)	खोल्या (kholyā) rooms
खुर्ची (khurchee)	खुर्च्या (khurchyā) chairs

(vi) Neutral nouns ending in a consonant are converted into their plurals by adding े (e) to the consonant. Examples :

Sing.	*Pl.*
घर (ghar)	घरे (ghare) houses
झाड़ (jhāḍ)	झाड़े (jhāḍe) trees
दार (dār)	दारे (dāre) doors

—: o :—

CHAPTER 3

VERBS

Let us first study the pronouns. In Marāthi, as in other Indian languages, there exists a special form of pronoun, which one uses when referring to or addressing a person to whom respect is due.

Marāthi pronouns may be listed as follows :

Singular	*Plural*
I=mee मी	We=āmhee आम्ही
You too तू (familiar) tumhee तुम्ही (respectful)	You tumhee तुम्ही (fam.) tumhee तुम्ही (resp.)
He to तो (fam.) te ते (resp.)	They te ते (fam.) te ते (resp.)
She tee ती (fam) tyā त्या (resp.)	They tyā त्या (fam.) tyā त्या (resp.)
It=te ते	They=tee ती

A Marāthi verb-form (infinite) has the ending ṇe (णे) appended to its stem or root For instance,

बोल-णे	bola-ṇe	=	to speak, to talk
खा-णे	khā-ṇe	=	to eat
जा-णे	jā-ṇe	=	to go
ये-णे	ye-ṇe	=	to come
अस-णे	asa-ṇe	=	to be, etc,

Marathi verbs are conjugated by adding to their roots or stems different suffixes, according to the tense and the gender, so also the number (singular and plural) of the noun.

A verb is conjugated as follows :

Note that all suffixes like to, tos, etc. are appended to the stem or root bola—. Suffixes are given in **bold**. The corresponding negative form are given at the end of each chart of conjugation. For instance : mee bola**t** nāhee would be the negative form of mee bola**to**.

बोलणे

bolaṇe=to speak, to talk

Present Tense

I talk

sing. mee [1]bola**to** मी बोलतो (masculine)
mee [1]bola**te** मी बोलते (feminine)

pl *We talk*=āmhee [1]bola**to** आम्ही बोलतो

You talk

too [2]bola**tos** तू बोलतोस (familiar/masculine)
sing. too [2]bola**tes** तू बोलतेस (familiar/feminine)
tumhee [1]bola**tā** तुम्ही बोलता (resp./mas.)
tumbee [1]bola**tā** तुम्ही बोलता (resp./fem.)

pl. *You talk*=tumhee [1]bola**tā** तुम्ही बोलता

He talks

sing to bola**to** तो बोलतो (familiar)
te [3]bola**tāt** ते बोलतात (respectful)

pl. *They talk*=te [3]bola**tāt** ते बोलतात

She talks

sing. tee [1]bolate ती बोलते (familiar)

tyā [3]bolatāt त्या बोलतात (respectful)

pl. *They talk*=tyā [3]bolatāt त्या बोलतात

sing. *It talks*=te [1]bolate ते बोलते

pl. *They talk*=tee [3]bolatāt ती बोलतात

Negative Forms

1. bolat nāhee 2. bolat nāhees 3. bolat nāheet

—: o :—

बोलणे

bolaṇe = to speak, to talk

Past Tense

I talked

sing. **mee** [1]**bolalo** मी बोललो (masculine)
mee [1a]**bolale** मी बोलले (feminine)

pl. *We talked* = āmhee [1]**bolalo** आम्ही बोललो

You talked

too [2]**bolalās** तू बोललास (mas.) (familiar)
sing. too [2a]**bolalees** तू बोललीस (fem.) („)
tumhee [3]**bolalāt** तुम्ही बोललात (mas) (resp.)
tumhee [3]**bolalāt** तुम्ही बोललात (fem.) („)

pl. *You talked* = tumhee [2]**bolalāt** तुम्ही बोललात

He talked

sing. to [4]**bolalā** तो बोलला (familiar)
te [4a]**bolale** ते बोलले (respectful)

pl. *They talked* = te [4a]**bolale** ते बोलले

She talked

sing. tee [5]bolalee ती बोलली (familiar)
tyā [5a]bolalyā त्या बोलल्या (respectful)

pl. *They talked*=tyā [5a]bolalyā त्या बोलल्या

sing. *It talked*=te [1a]bolale ते बोलले

pl. *They talked*=tee [6]bolalee ती बोलली

Negative Forms

1. bolalo nāhee
1a. bolale nāhee
2. bolalā nāhees
2a. bolalee nāhees
3. bolalā rāheet
4. bolalā nāhee
4a. bolale nāheet
5. bolalee nāhee
5a. bolalyā nāheet
6. bolalee nāheet

—: o :—

बोलणे

bolaṇe = to speak, to talk

Future Tense

Suffixes of the future tense in Marāthi are the same for all the genders.

sing. *I will talk* = mee [1]**bolen** मी बोलेन

pl. *We will talk* = āmhee [1]**boloo** आम्ही बोलू

You will talk

sing. too [2]**bolsheel** तू बोलशील (familiar)

tumhee [3]**bolāl** तुम्ही बोलाल (respectful)

pl. *You will talk* = tumhee [1]**bolāl** तुम्ही बोलाल

He will talk

sing. to [1]**bolel** तो बोलेल (fam.)

te [3]**bolteel** ते बोलतील (resp.)

pl. *They will talk* = te [3]**bolteel** ते बोलतील

She will talk

sing. **tee [1]bolel** ती बोलेल (fam.)

tyā [3]bolteel त्या बोलतील (resp.)

pl. *They will talk*=tyā **bolteel** त्या बोलतील

sing. *It will talk*=te [1]**bolel** ते बोलेल

pl. *They will talk*=tee [1]**bolteel** ती बोलतील

Negative Forms

1. **bolnār** nāhee
2. **bolnār** nāhees
3. **bolnār** nāheet

—: o :—

In most languages, Indian as well as foreign, the verbs '*to be*' is conjugated independent of the rules applicable to other verbs. In other words, the verb '*to be*' is irregular in its conjugation. This is also true of the Marāthi verb asaṇe.

असणे

asaṇe=to be

Present Tense

sing. *I am*=meẹ [1]āhe
pl. *We are*=āmhee [1]āhot

sing. *You are*=too [2]āhes (fam.)
tumhee [1]āhāt (resp.)
pl. *You are*=tumhee [1]āhāt

sing. *He is*=to [1]āhe (fam.)/te [3]āhet (resp.)
pl. *They are*=te [3]āhet

sing. *She is*=tee [1]āhe (fam.)/tyā [3]āhet (resp.)
pl. *They are*=tyā [3]āhet

sing. *It is*=te [1]āhe
pl. *They are*=tee [3]āhet

Negative Forms

1. nāhee 2. nāhees 3. nāheet

असणे

asaṇe=to be

Past Tense

sing. *I was*=mee [1]hoto
pl. *We were*=āmhee [1]hoto

sing. *You were*=tu [2]hotas (mas.) (familiar)
tu [2a]hotees (fem.) (,,)
tumhee [3]hotā (mas.) (respectful)
tumhee [3]hotā (fem.) (,,)
pl. *You were*=tumhee [3]hotā

sing. *He was*=to [3]hotā (familiar)
te [4]hote (respectful)
pl. *They were*=te [4]hote

sing. *She was*=tee [5]hoti (familiar)
tyā [6]hotyā (respectful)
pl. *They were*=tyā [6]hotyā

sing. *It was*=te [4]hote
pl. *They were*=tee [5]hotee

Negative Forms

1. navhato	4. navhate
2. navhatās	5 navhatee
2a. navhatees	6. navhatyā
3. navhatā	

—: o :—

असणे

asaṇe=to be

Future Tense

sing. *I shall be*=mee [1]asen

pl. *We shall be*=āmhee [6]asoo

sing. *You will be*=too [2]asasheel (mas.) (fam.)
too [3]asasheel (fem.) (fam.)
tumhee [3]asāl (mas.) (resp.)
tumhee [2]asāl (fem) (resp.)

pl. *You will be*=tumhee [3]asāl

sing. *He will be*=to [4]asel (fam.)
te [5]asateel (resp.)

pl. *They will be*=te [5]asateel

sing. *She will be*=tee [4]asel (fam.)
tyā [5]asateel (resp.)

pl. *They will be*=tyā [5]asateel

sing. *It will be*=te [4]asel

pl. *They will be*=tee [5]asateel

Negative Forms

1. nasen
2. nasasheel
3. nasāl
4. nasel
5. nasateel
6. nasoo

—: o :—

Having studied the conjugation of typical Marāthi verb bolaṇe in the present, past and future tenses, we shall now examine how it is conjugated in its continuous and perfect tenses.

Its conjugated forms in these tenses are composed of the root bolat, coupled with the corresponding form of the verb asaṇe, which acts as an auxiliary verb to form these tenses.

बोलणे

bolaṇe = to speak, to talk

Present Continuous Tense

sing. *I am talking* = mee bolat [1]ahe

pl. *We are talking* = āmhee bolat [1]āhot

sing. *You are talking* = too bolat [2]āhes (fam.)
tumhee bolat [1]āhāt (resp.)

pl. *You are talking* = tumhee bolat [1]āhāt

sing. *He is talking* = to bolat [1]āhe (fam,)
te bolat [3]āhet (resp.)

pl. *They are talking* = te bolat [3]āhet

sing. *She is talking*=tee bolat [1]āhe (fam.)
tyā bolat [3]āhet (resp.)
pl. *They are talking*=tyā bolat [3]āhet

sing. *It is talking*=te bolat [1]āhe
pl. *They are talking*=tee bolat [3]āhet

Negative Forms

1. nāhee   2. nāhees   3. nāheet

—: o :—

बोलणे

bolaṇe=to speak, to talk

Past Continuous Tense

sing. *I was talking*=mee bolat [1]hoto

pl. *We were talking*=āmhee bolat [1]hoto

sing. *You were talking*=too bolat [2]hotas (mas.)/ (fam.)
too bolat [3]hotees (fem.) (fam.)
tumhee bolat [4]hotā (mas.) (resp.)
tumhee bolat [4]hota (fem.) (resp.)

pl. *You were talking*=tumhee bolat [4]hotā

sing. *He was talking*=to bolat [4]hotā (fam.)
te bolat [5]hote (resp.)

pl. *They were talking*=te bolat [5]hote

sing. *She was talking*=tee bolat [6]hotee (fam.)
tyā bolat [7]hotyā (resp.)

pl. *They were talking*=tyā bolat [7]hotyā

sing. *It was talking*=te bolat [5]hote

pl. *They were talking*=tee bolat [6]hotee

Negative Forms

1. navhato
2. navhatās
3. navhatees
4. navhatā
5. navhate
6. navhatee
7. navhatyā

—: o :—

बोलणे

bolaṇe=to speak, to talk

Present Perfect Tense

sing. *I have talked*=mee bolalo [1]āhe
pl *We have talked*=āmhee bolalo [1]āhot

sing. *You have talked*=too bolalā [2]āhes (mas.)
too bolalee [1]āhes (fem.) (fam.) (fam.)
tumhee bolalā [3]āhāt (mas.) (resp.)
tumhee bolalā [3]āhāt (fem.) (resp.)
pl. *You have talked*=tumhee bolalā [3]āhāt

sing. *He has talked*=to bolalā [1]āhe (fam.)
te bolale [3]āhet (resp.)
pl. *They have talked*=te bolale [3]āhet

sing. *She has talked*=tee bolalee [1]āhe (fam.)
tyā bolalyā [3]āhet (resp.)
pl. *They have talked*=tyā bolalyā [3]āhet

sing *It has talked*=te bolale ^{1}āhe

pl. *They have talked*=tee bolalee ^{3}āhet

Negative Forms

1. nāhee 2. nāhees 3. nāheet

—: o :—

बोलणे

bolaṇe = to speak, to talk

Past Perfect Tense

sing. *I had talked* = mee bolalo [1]hoto
pl. *We had talked* = āmhee bolalo [1]hoto

sing. *You had talked* = too bolalā [2]hotās (mas.)
too bolalee [3]hotees (fem) (fam.) **(fam.)**
tumhee bolalā [4]hotā (mas.) (resp.)
tumee bolalā [4]hota (fem.) (resp.)
pl. *You had talked* = tumhee bolalā [4]hotā

sing. *He had talked* = to bolalā [4]hotā (fam.)
te bolale [5]hote (resp.)
pl. *They had talked* = te bolale [5]hote

sing. *She had talked* = tee bolalee [6]hotee (fam.)
tyā bolalyā [7]hotyā (resp.)
pl. *They had talked* = tyā bolalyā [7]hotyā

sing. *It had talked* = te bolale [5]hote
pl. *They had talked* = tee bolalee [6]hotee

Negative Forms

1. navhato
2. navhatās
3. navhatees
4. navhatā
5. navhate
6. navhatee
7. navhatyā

—: o :—

CHAPTER 4

CASES

They are :

I The Nominative Case

प्रथमा विभक्ति

Prathamā Vibhakti

(1) The nom which stands for subject does not take any suffix in any of the tenses or moods when the verb is intransitive.

Sing.	*Pl.*
Ghodā dhāvto	Ghode dhāvtāt
(a horse runs)	(horses run)
Ghodee dhāvte	Ghodee dhāvtāt
(a mare runs)	(mares run)

(2) The same rule applies even to transitive verbs except in the past tense.

Ghodā gavat khāto

(a horse eats grass)

However, when the transitive verb is in the past tense, the suffix **ne** is added to the subject. Hence

Ghodyā**ne** gavat khālle
(a hoı se ate the grass)

II The Accusative or Objective Case

द्वितीया विभक्ति

Dwitteeyā Vibhakti

When functioning as an object, the noun takes the suffix **sa** and/or **lā** in the singular, and **nā** in the plural.

Rām vidyārthyā**n**ā shikavito*
(Ram teaches pupils)

Rām vidyārthyālā or vidyārthyā**sa** shikavito
(Ram teaches a pupil)

However, the object does not take any suffix when ths verb describes the act of eating, drinking or driving. Thus,

Rām āmbā khāto.
(Ram eats a mango)

Rām pānee pito.
(Ram drinks water)

Rām gāḍee *chālvito.
(Ram drives a car)

The Causative :

*shikaṇe=to learn; but shikaviṇe=to teach.
chālaṇe=to walk, to move; but, chālaviṇe=to drive. Similarly,
jhopaṇe=to sleep; jhopaviṇe=to put to sleep.
radaṇe=to weep; radaviṇe=to cause to weep.

III The Instrumental Case

तृतीया विभक्ति

Triteeya Vibhakti

Its suffixes known as *pratyays* are as follows :

Sing.	*Pl.*
ने (ne)=by/with	नी (nee)=by
शी (shee)=with	शी (shee)=with

मी सुरीने आंबा कापतो.
mee suree*ne* āmbā kāpato.
I cut a mango with a knife.

ते सुऱ्यांनी आंबे कापतात.
te suryā*nee* āmbe kāpatāt.
They cut mangoes with knives.

मी मुलाशी बोलतो.
mee mulā*shee* bolato.
I talk with a boy.

मी मुलांशी बोलतो.
mee mulān*shee* bolato.
I talk with boys.

IV The Dative Case

चतुर्थी विभक्ति

Chaturthee Vibhakti

Suffixes for the dative case are :

Sing.	*Pl.*
स (sa) = for, to	ना (nā) = for, to
ला (lā) = for, to	

माझ्या बायकोस/बायकोला दागिने फार आवडतात.
mazyā bāyakō*sa*/bāyakō*lā* dāgine phār āwadatāt.
My wife is very fond of ornaments.
(*Literally* : to my wife, ornaments are very pleasing.)

मी त्यांना काय सांगु ?
mee tyā*nā* kāy sāngu ?
What shall I tell them ?

V The Ablative Case

पंचमी विभक्ति

Panchamee Vibhakti

Suffixes in this case are common for singular and plural. They are :

पासून (pāsoon) = from   तून (toon) = from
हुन (hoon) = from (a city).

Examples :

घरापासून शेत चार मैल दूर आहे.
gharā*pāsoon* shet chār maeel door āhe.
The farm is four miles away from the house.

ती दवाखान्यातुन पाच वाजता घरी येते.

tee dawākhānyā*toon* pāch wājatā gharee yete.

She comes home from the dispensary at five o'clock.

तु कानपुरहुन केंव्हा परत आलास ?
tu Kānpur*hoon* kenvhā parat ā ās ?
When did you return from Kanpur ?

VI Possessive Case

षष्ठी विभक्ति

Shashthee Vibhakti

Its suffixes are :

Sing.	*Pl.*
mas. चा (chā)	mas. चे (che)
fem. ची (chee)	fem. च्या (chyā)
neu. चे (che)	neu ची (chee)

As the term 'possessive' indicates, this case corresponds to the English 'of' or the apostrophe sign attached to a noun. In Marathi, the suffix changes according to the gender of the noun which follows it.

Examples :

Sing. मुलाचा/मुलीचा चेहरा (mas.)

mulā*chā*/mulee*chā* chehrā

Boy's/Girl's face

Pl. मुलांचे/मुलींचे चेहरे

mulān*che* muleen*che* chehre

Boys /Girls' faces

Sing. मुलाची/मुलीची सायकल (fem.)

mulā*chee*/mulee*chee* saikal

Boy's/Girl's cycle

Pl. मुलांच्या/मुलींच्या सायकली

mulān*chyā*/muleen*chyā* saikalee

Boys'/Girls' cycles

Sing. मुलाचे/मुलीचे पुस्तक (neu.)
mulā*che*/mulee*che* pustak
Boy's/Girl's book

Pl. मुलांची/मुलींची पुस्तके
mulān*chee*/muleen*chee* pustake
Boys'/Girls' books

VII The Locative Case

सप्तमी विभक्ति

Saptamee Vibhakti

Its suffixes too are common for singular and plural. They are :

आत (āt)=in, into, inside

ईत (eet)=in, into, inside

वर (var)=on, upon

Examples :

घरात कोणी नाही.

ghar*āt* koṇee nāhee.

No one is in the house.

पिशवित दाढ़ीचे सामान आहे.

pishav*eet* dāḍheeche sāmān āhe.

There is a shaving kit in the bag,

चहात साखर नाही.
chah*āt* sākhar nāhee.
There is no sugar in the tea.

पलंगावर गादी आहे.
palangā*var* gādee āhe.
There's a mattress on the cot.

आत या ना.
āt yā nā.
Do come inside.

VIII The Vocative Case

संबोधन विभक्ति

Sambodhan Vibhakti

As in English, this case is used when calling a person. In Marathi, there are two different prefixes, one familiar and the other formal.

Familiar	*Formal*
अरे ! (aray !)	अहो ! (aho) !
अे ! (ae !)	

They correspond to the English He ! and and Hallo ! respectively, and are common for both the sexes.

Examples :

अरे, तु येथे काय करतोस ?
aray, tu yeṭhe kāy kartos ?
Hey, what are you doing here ?

अहो, जरा बाहेर येता का ?
aho, jarā bāher yetā kā ?
Hello, won't you come out for a while ?

Some transitive verbs take two objects, a direct and an indirect one. The direct object does not take any suffix, while the indirect object takes the suffixes **sa** and/or **lā** in the singular and **nā** in the plural.

Rām mitrā**sa**/**lā** patra leehito.
(Ram writes a letter to a friend)

Rām jhādā**sa**/**lā** pāni ghālato.
(Ram waters a tree)

—: o :—

The Use of Prepositions

(i) *with*

The preposition with is represented by the Marathi suffix **ne.** For instance,

mee lekhaṇee**ne** leehito.
(I write with a pen)

(ii) *for*

Represented by the Marathi suffix **kareetā** or **sāthee.**

mee mitrā**kareetā** or **mitrāsāthee** pustak vikat gheto.
(I buy a book for a friend)

(iii) *of*

Represented by **chā** (masculine), **chee** (feminine) and **che** (neuter). The corresponding plural forms of the suffixes are **che** (mas.), **chyā** (fem.) and **chee** (neut). Thus,

Sing.	*Pl.*
Rām**chā** bhāu	Rām**che** bhāu
(Ram's brother)	(Ram's brothers)

Sing.	*Pl.*
Rāmchee baheeṇa (Ram's sister)	Rāmchyā baheeṇee (Ram's sisters)
Rāmche pustak (Ram's book)	Rāmchee pustake (Ram's books)

(iv) *in*

Represented by **āt**

ghar**āt** mule āhet.

(Children are in the house)

(v) *out*

Represented by **bāher**

gharā**bāher** bāg āhe.

(There is a garden outside the house)

(vi) *above/on*

Represented by **var**

gharā**var** kavle āhet.

(There are tiles above the house)

(vii) *below/under*

Represented by **khālee**

jhādā**khālee** nehamee sāvlee *asate.

(There is always shade under a tree)

[*asate (asatāt, plural) as against āhe (āhet, plural) is a special form of the verb asaṇe=to be —which is used to state a universal truth.]

(viii) *near/near to*

Represented by **pāshee, javal, shejāree**

pulā**javal** kār ubhee āhe.

(There is a car parked—standing near a bridge)

(ix) *in front of*

Represented by **puḍhe, samor**

dukānā**puḍhe** gardee jamalee āhe.

(A crowd has gathered in front of a shop)

(x) *behind*

Represented by **māge**

imārateе**māge** nadee āhe.

(There is a river behind the building)

(xi) *from/since*

Represented by **pāsoon**

kāl**pāsoon** paoos padat āhe.

(It has been raining since yesterday)

(xii) *along with*

Represented by **barobar**

mazyā**barobar** yetos kā ?

(Will you come with me ?)

(xiii) *without*

Represented by **vāchoon, shivāy**

dnyānāvāchoon māṇasāche jeevan vyartha āhe.
(Man's life is worthless without knowledge)

pānyā**shivāy** māse jagu shakaṇār nāheet.
(Fish will not be able to live without water)

(xiv) *to, towards*

Represented by **kade**
tee maitreeṇee**kade** jāt āhe.
(She is going to a girl-friend's house)

(xv) *because of*

Represented by **mule**
pāwasā**mule** āj khel jhālā nāhee.
(There was no play today because of rain)

(xvi) *instead of*

Represented by **eiwajee**

phulā**eiwajee** phale kā āṇalees ?

(Why did you bring fruits instead of flowers ?)

—: o :—

Following are the masculine, feminine and neuter forms, respectively, of the pronouns I, you, etc.

sing. my/mine
(māzā, māzee, māze)

pl. *our/ours
(āmchā, āmchee, āmche)

sing your (s)
(tuzā, tuzee, tuze) familiar
(tumchā, tumchee, tumche) respectful

pl. (tumchā, tumchee, tumche)

sing. his
(tyāchā, tyāchee, tyāche) familiar
(tyānchā, tyānchee, tyānche) respectful

pl. their (s)
(tyānchā, tyānchee, tyānche)

sing. her (s)
(teechā, teechee, teeche) familiar
(tyānchā, tyānchee, tyānche) respectful

pl. their (s)
(tyānchā, tyānchee, tyānche)

sing. its

(tyāchā, tyāchee, tyāche)

pl. their (s)

(tyānchā, tyānchee, tyānche)

āplā, āplee, āple are the special forms of our(s). They are used when the speaker wants to include the person (s) he is talking to, For instance, a father showing his children a newly bought house would say : he āple nave ghar ! However, to a guest he would say : he āmche nave ghar.

—: o :—

CHAPTER 5

ADJECTIVES

In Marathi, there are *two* types of adjectives, namely, **invariable** and **variable.**

Invariable Adjectives

These are adjectives which do not change their forms according to the gender and number (sing. or plural) of the noun they qualify. Such adjectives usually end in *ee* or *oo*. For instance :

(i) मऊ, maoo = soft

Singular	*Plural*
ooshee maoo āhe.	ooshyā maoo āhet
(the pillow is soft)	(pillows are soft)
ऊशी मऊ आहे.	ऊश्या मऊ आहेत.

(ii) चौकोनी, chaukonee = rectangular

pustak chaukonee āhe.	pustake chaukonee āhet
(the book is rectangular)	(books are rectangular)
पुस्तक चौकोनी आहे.	पुस्तके चौकोनी आहेत.

Sometimes such adjectives end in a consonant.

(iii) हुशार, hushār=clever, intelligent

mulagā hushār āhe.	mulage hushār āhet.
(the boy is clever)	(boys are clever)
मुलगा हुशार आहे.	मुलगे हुशार आहेत.

(iv) ऊंच, ooncha=tall

ghar ooncha āhe.	ghare ooncha āhet.
(the house is tall)	(houses are tall)
घर ऊंच आहे.	घरे ऊंच आहेत.

Some other invariable adjectives :

jad (heavy), naveen (new), mahāg (costly), saral (straight), thengu (short), lāl (red), gol (round), sukhee (happy), dukhee (unhappy), gulābee (pink).

Singular/Plural

mas. lāl diva, red lamp/lāl dive.
fem. lāl sādee, red saree/lāl saḍyā.
neu. lāl pustak, red book/lāl pustake.
mas. gulābee paḍada, pink curtain/ gulābee paḍade.
fem. gulābee chādar, pink bed sheet/ gulābee chadaree.
neu. gulābee phul, pink flower/gulābee phule.

Variable Adjectives

If a variable adjective ends in *ā* (for instance, pāndharā, पांढरा=white), its feminine form ends in *ee* (pāndharee, पांढरी) and the neuter form in *e* (pāndhare, पांढरे). Thus,

mas. pāndharā ghoḍa, a white horse.
fem. pāndharee ghoḍee, a white mare.
neu. pāndhare phul, a white flower.

Their corresponding plural forms would be :

mas. pāndhare ghoḍe.
fem. pāndharyā ghoḍyā.
neu. pāndharee phule.

Hence it may be noted that the plural forms of adjectives are formed according to the following rules :

mas. the ending *ā* is replaced by *e* (आ→ए).
fem. the ending *ee* is replaced by *yā* (ई→या).
neu. the ending *e* is replaced by *ee* (ए→ई).

Comparative and Superlative Degrees

Unlike English, Marathi has no suffixes corresponding to *—er* and *—est*, denoting the comparative and superlative degrees, respectively. Instead the suffix *peksha* (पेक्षा) is used for the comparative and *sarvāt* (सर्वांत) for the superlative degree. The suffix *itakā* (इतका) or *yewaḍhā* (येवढा) would indicate the positive degree.

Rām Gopāl itakā ooncha āhe.

राम गोपाल इतका ऊंच आहे.

Ram is as tall as Gopal.

Parantu (or paṇ) Kiron Arun pekshā ooncha āhe.

परंतु-पण किरण अरुण पेक्षा ऊंच आहे.

But Kiron is taller than Arun.

Himalaya parvat sarvāt ooncha āhe.

हिमालय पर्वत सर्वात ऊंच आहे.

The Himalaya is the tallest of all mountains.

Ordinal Adjectives

Number	*Adjective*
ek (one)	pahilā (first)
don (two)	dusarā (second)
teen (three)	tisarā (third)
chār (four)	chauthā (fourth)

From five (pānch) onwards, the ordinal adjectives are formed by adding the suffix **wā** (वा) to the cardinal numbers. For instance,

Number	*Adjective*
pāncha (five)	pānchwā (fifth)
sahā (six)	sahāwā (sixth)
sāt (seven)	sātwā (seventh)
āṭh (eight)	āṭhwā (eighth)

and so on upto eighteen.

aṭharā (eighteen)	aṭharāwā (eighteenth)

From nineteenth onwards, the word *ā* (आ) is inserted between the cardinal number and the suffix *wā* (वा).

ekoṇees (nineteen)	ekoṇeesāwā (nineteenth)
wees (twenty)	weesāwā (twentieth)
ekwees (twentyone)	ekweesāwā (twentyfirst)

and so on.

All the ordinal adjectives are variable and they follow the rules governing the variable adjectives. For instance :

Singular	*Plural*
mas :	
pahilā dhaḍa	pahile dhaḍe
(first lesson)	(first lessons)
पहिला धडा	पहिले धडे

fem :

pahilee vidyārthinee	pahilyā vidyārthinee
(first girl-student)	(first girl-students)
पहिली विद्यार्थिनी	पहिल्या विद्यार्थिनी

neu :

pahile mul	pahilee mule
(first child)	(first children)
पहिले मुल	पहिली मुले

Following are the coordinate conjunctions which join two words or two clauses :

— *āṇi/wa* (and)

Ram āṇi Rahim māze mitra āhet.
Ram and Rahim are my friends.

— *kinwā* (or)

āj kinwā udyā mee tulā bheten.
I shall meet you today or tomorrow.

— *parantu/paṇa* (but, however)

malā Marathi wāchatā yete, parantu ajoon liheetā yet nāhi.

I can read Marathi, but cannot write it yet.

— *mhaṇoon* (therefore, hence)

teelā kāl bare wāṭat navhate, mhaṇoon tee shālet gelee nāhi.

She was not feeling well yesterday; hence she did not go to school.

— *kāraṇ* (because)

malā Marāthi shikaṇyāchee ichchhā āhe,kāraṇ malā Mahārashṭrāt nokaree karāyachee āhe.
I wish to learn Marathi, because I want to take up a job in Maharashtra.

— *sud-ḍhā* (also, too)

March maheenyāt sud-ḍhā Dillit bareech thanḍi asate.

In March too, Delhi is quite cold.

— *ne* (by, by means of)

āmhee busne pravās karṇār āhot.

We shall be travelling by bus.

— *kharokhar* (indeed)

tu pās zālās, hee kharokhar ānandāchee goshṭa āhe.

It is indeed a happy event that you have passed.

— *fakta* (only)

fakta tyā yewoo shakalyā naheet.

Only she (resp.) could not come.

— *jar...tar* (if...then)

tu jar ravivāree māzyākaḍe yesheel (ālās) tar āpaṇa doghe nāṭakālā jāwoo.

If you come to me on Sunday, (then) we (both of us) shall go to (see) a play.

— *jaree...taree* (even if)

jaree pustak mahāg asle, taree mee te wikat ghe-een.

Even if the book is costly, I shall buy it.

—: o :—

Interrogative Pronouns

— *kuṭhe* (where)

tumhee kuṭhe rāhātā ?

Where do you stay/live ?

— *kenwhā* (when)

tumchee shālā kenwhā suṭate ?

When does your school close ?

— *jenwhā...tenwhā* (when...then)

jenwhā shevaṭachee ghanṭā hote, tenwhā āmchee shālā suṭate

When the last bell goes, (then) our school closes.

— *kāy* (what)

he kāy āhe ?
What is this ?

— *kitee* (how much, how many)

ṭeblāwar kitee pustake āhet ?
How many books are there on the table ?

— *kase* (how)

tumhee kase āhāt ?
How are you ?

— *kā* (why)

tulā wel kā zālā ?
Why are you late ?

— *koṇa* (who)

tumache adhyāpak koṇa āhet ?
Who is your headmaster ?

— *koṇchā* (*—chee, —che*) (which)

koṇche shahar (neu.) tulā jāsta āwoḍate ?
Which city do you like more ?

— *koṇāchā* (*—chee, —che*) (whose)

hee jameen (fem.) koṇāchee āhe ?
Whose land is this ?

—: o :—

Syntax

Marathi sentences are formed according to following sequences :

(1) The subject should precede the verb.

to roj vyāyam karato.
He takes exercise every day.

(2) The object should follow the subject but precede the verb.

mee āmbā khāto.
I eat a mango.

(3) The indirect object should immediately precede the direct object.

mee mitrālā wahee deto.
I give a friend a notebook.

(4) The adjective should immediately precede the noun.

mee goḍ āmbā khato.
I eat a sweet mango.

(5) The adverb should immediately precede the verb.

tee jalad chālate.
She walks fast.

—: o :—

CHAPTER 6

NUMBERS

अंक

(Anka)

The numbers one to nine are :

अेक ek	one	सहा sahā	six
दोन don	two	सात sāt	seven
तीन teen	three	आठ āṭh	eight
चार chār	four	नअु na-oo	nine
पाच pāch	five		

The number ten and its multiples are :

दहा dahā	ten	साठ sāth	sixty
वीस vees	twenty	सत्तर sattar	seventy
तीस tees	thirty	अैंशी ainshee	eighty
चाळीस chālees	forty	नव्वद nav-vad	ninety
पन्नास pannās	fifty	शंभर shāmbhar	hundred

हजार hajār	a thousand
दहा हजार dahā hajār	ten thousand
लाख lākh	a lakh
दहा लाख dahā lākh	ten lakhs

We shall now see how ordinals are formed in Marathi. Being adjectives, they take the adjectival endings, according to the gender of the nouns they qualify. This is also true of the cases, singular and/or plural.

Number		*Ordinal*	
one	अेक ek	first	पहिला pahilā
two	दोन don	second	दुसरा dusarā
three	तीन teen	third	तीसरा teesarā
four	चार chār	fourth	चौथा chauthā
five	पाच pāch	fifth	पाचवा pāchavā
six	सहा sahā	sixth	सहावा sahāvā
seven	सात sāt	seventh	सातवा sātavā
eight	आठ āṭh	eighth	आठवा āṭhavā
nine	नअु na-oo	ninth	नववा navavā
ten	दहा dahā	tenth	दहावा dahāwā

Note that from the number five onwards, the corresponding ordinals are formed by the suffix वा (*vā*), वी (*vee*), and वे (*ve*) are its feminine and neuter counterparts respectively, while वी (*vee*) is the common plural suffix This rule governing the ordinals of Marathi numbers is applicable to numbers five to infinity. Thus, akarā (eleven), akarāvā, akarāvee, akarāve (eleventh)...

The numbers eleven to ninetynine are :

11 अकरा
akarā

12 बारा
bārā

13 तेरा
terā

14 चौदा
chaudā

15 पंधरा
pandharā

16 सोळा
solā

17 सतरा
satarā

18 अठरा
aṭharā

19 अेकोणीस
ekoṇees

20 वीस
vees

21 अेकवीस
ekvees

22 बावीस
bāvees

23 तेवीस
tevees

24 चोवीस
chovees

25 पंचवीस
panchvees

26 सव्वीस
savvees

27 सत्तावीस
sattāvees

28 अठ्ठावीस
aṭhāvees

29 अेकोणतीस
ekoṇtees

30 तीस
tees

31 अेकतीस
ektees

32 बत्तीस
battees

33 तेहेतीस
tehetees

34 चौतीस
chautees

35 पस्तीस
pastees

36 छत्तीस
chhattees

37 सदोतीस
sadotees

38 अडोतीस
adotees

39 अेकोणचाळीस
ekoṇchalees

40 चाळीस
chālees

41 अेकेचाळीस
ekechālees

42 बेचाळीस
bechālees

43 त्रेचाळीस
trechālees

44 चव्वेचाळीस
chavve chālees

45 पंचेचाळीस
panche chālees

46 सेहेचाळीस
sehe chālees

47 सत्तेचाळीस
satte chālees

48 अट्ठेचाळीस
aṭhe chālees

49 अेकुणपन्नास
ekun pannās

50 पन्नास
pannās

51 अेकावन
ekāvan

52 बावन
bavan

53 त्रेपन
trepan

54 चोपन
chopan

55 पंचावन
panchāvan

56 छप्पन
chhappan

57 सत्तावन
sattavan

58 अठ्ठावन
aṭhavan

59 अेकुणसाठ
ekuṇsāth

60 साठ
sāṭh

61 अेकसष्ठ
ek sashtha

62 बासष्ठ
ba sashtha

63 त्रेसष्ठ
tresashtha

64 चौसष्ठ
chousashtha

65 पासष्ठ
pasashtha

66 सहासष्ठ
sahāsashtha

67 सदुसष्ठ
sadusashtha

68 अडुसष्ठ
adusashtha

69 अेकुणसत्तरे
ekunsattar

70 सत्तर
sattar

71 अेकाहत्तर
ekāhttar

72 बहात्तर
bahāttar

73 त्र्यहात्तर
tryahāttar

74 चौर्‍याहत्तर
chauryāhattar

75 पंचाहत्तर
panchāhattar

76 शहात्तर
shahattar

77 सत्त्याहत्तर
sattyāhattar

78 अठ्याहत्तर
aṭhāhattar

79 अेकुणअैंशी
ekuṇaishee

80 एंशी
ainshee

81 अेक्यांशी
ekkyānshee

82 ब्यायंशी
byānshee

83 त्र्यायंशी
tryānshee

84 चौर्‍यायंशी
chauryānshee

85 पंच्यायंशी
panchyānshee

86 शहायंशी
shahayānshee

87 सत्त्यायंशी
sattyānshee

88 अठ्ठायंशी
aṭhyānshee

89 अेकुणनव्वद
ekunnavvad

90 नव्वद
navvad

91 अेक्याणव
ekyaṇav

92 ब्याणव
byaṇav

93 त्र्याणव
tryāṇav

94 चौऱ्याणव
chauryāṇav

95 पंच्याणव
panchyāṇav

96 शहाण्णव
shahāṇav

97 सत्त्याण्णव
sattyāṇav

98 अठ्ठाण्णव
aṭhyāṇav

99 नव्याणव
navyāṇav

The number 100 and its multiples are :

100 शंभर
shambhar

200 दोनशे
donshe

300 तीनशे
teenshe

400 चारशे
chārshe

500 पाचशे
pāchshe

600 सहाशें
sahashe

700 सातशें
sātshe

800 आठशे
āṭhshe

900 नऊशे
naushe

The numbers from 101 onwards are :

101 अेकशे अेक
ekshe ek

102 अेंकशे दोन
ekshe don

103	अेकशे तीन ekshe teen	108	अेकशे आठ ekshe āṭh
104	अेकशे चार ekshe chār	109	अेकशे नअु ekshe nau
105	अेकशे पाच ekshe pāch	110	अेकशे दहा ekshe dahā
106	अेकशे सहा ekshe sahā	111	अेकशे अकरा ekshe akarā
107	अेकशे सात ekshe sāt		

203	दोनशे तीन	867	आठशे सदुमष्ठ
306	तीनशे सहा	999	नअुशे नव्याणव
415	चारशे पंधरा	1225	अेक हजार दोनशे पंचवीस
527	पाचशे सत्तावीस	3420	तीन हजार चारशे वीस

—: o :—

Part II—Language

LESSON 1

किती वाजले ?
Kitee Wājale ?
What's the time ?

आता सकाळचे नऊ वाजले आहेत.
ātā sakālche nau wājale āhet.
It is now nine o'clock in the morning.

नऊ वाजून दहा मिनीटांनी मी घरा बाहेर पडेन.
nau wājoon dahā mineeṭānee mee gharābāher paḍen.
I shall leave house at ten minutes past nine.

आणी साडे नऊ वाजता ऑफिसात पोहोचेन.
āṇee sāḍe nau wājatā offisāt pohochen.
And reach office at a half past nine.

सवा दहा वाजता पोस्टमन येतो.
sawā dahā wājatā postman yeto
At a quarter past ten, the postman comes.

पावणे अकरा वाजता आम्हाला चहा मिळतो.
pāwaṇe akrā wājatā āmhālā chahā milato.
We get tea at a quarter to eleven.

पाऊण ते सवा पर्यंत जेवणाची सुट्टी होते.
pāoon̤ te sawā paryant jewanāchee sut̤t̤i asate.
The lunch recess is from a quarter to one to a quarter past one.

दीड वाजता सर्व अधिकाऱ्यांची एक सभा होते.
deed̤ wājatā sarv adheekāryānchee ek sabhā hote.
At a half past one, all the officers assemble for a meeting.

सहा वाजता ऑफिस सुटते.
sahā wājatā office sut̤ate.
Office gets over at six o'clock.

—: o :—

LESSON 2

पुस्तकालय

विद्यार्थ्यांना अभ्यास करतांना अनेक पुस्तकांची आवश्यकता भासते.

परंतु सारी पुस्तके विकत घेणे त्यांना पैशाच्या अभावी शक्य नसते.

ह्या अडचणीतून मार्ग काढण्यासाठी पुस्तकालयांची योजना केलेली असते.

प्रत्येक विद्यालय, कॉलेज व कार्यालयात बहुधा पुस्तकालय असते.

पुस्तकालयात अनेक विषयावर पुस्तके असतात.

पुस्तकालयातील पुस्तके आठ किंवा पंधरा दिवसासाठी घरी नेता येतात.

परंतु ज्यां पुस्तकांची सर्वांना नेहमी आवश्यकता असते ती पुस्तके पुस्तकालयात वाचावी असा नियम असतो.

पुस्तकालयात अनेक भाषांची वर्तमानपत्रे देखिल येतात.

—: o :—

Pustakālay

Vidyārthyānā abhyās karatānā anek pustakānchee āwashyakatā bhāsate.

Parantu sāree pustake wikat gheṇe tyānā paishāchyā abhāwee shakya nasate.

Hyā aḍachaṇeetoon mārga kāḍhaṇyāsāṭhee pustakālayānchee yojanā kelelee asate.

Pratyek vidyālay, college, wa karyālay yat bahuḍhā pustakālay asate.

Pustakālayāt anek vishayāwar pustake asatāt.

Pustakālayāteel pustake āth kinwā pandharā diwasāsāṭhee gharee netā yetāt.

Parantu jyā pustakānchee sarvānā nehmee āwashyakatā asate tee pustake pustakālayātach wāchāwee asā niyam asato.

Pustakālayāt anek bhāshānchee vartamān-patre dekhil yetāt.

—: o :—

Library

When studying, students feel the need for several books.

However, they are unable to buy all the books due to lack of money.

In order to find a way out of this predicament, libraries are established.

In every school, college and office, there is usually a library.

There are books on several topics in a library.

Library books can be taken home for eight or ten days.

However, there is a rule that books which everyone always needs must be read in the library itself.

A library also receives newspapers in several languages.

—: o :—

LESSON 3

माझे घर

हे माझे घर आहे.

घरात ओसरी आहे.

ओसरीवर मुले बसली आहेत.

ओसरीच्या पलीकडे दिवाणखाना आहे.

दिवाणखान्यात टी.व्ही. आहे.

दिवाणखान्याच्या शेजारी झोपण्याची खोली आहे.

पाठीमागच्या बाजूला स्वयंपाकघर आहे.

घराच्या दुसऱ्या टोकाला न्हाणीघर आहे.

घराच्या पुढे व मागे अंगण आहे.

अंगणात बाग आहे.

बागेत फुलांची झाडे आहेत.

घरी वडील, आई, एक बहीण व दोन भाऊ आहेत

—: o :—

Maze Ghar

He māze ghar āhe.

Gharāt osaree āhe.

Osareewar mule basalee āhet.

Osareechyā paleekaḍe diwāṇkhānā āhe.

Diwāṇkhānyāt TV āhe.

Diwāṇkhāṇyachyā shejāree zopaṇyāchee kholee āhe.

Pātheemāgchyā bājoolā swayampākghar āhe.

Gharāchyā doosaryā tokālā nhāṇeeghar āhe.

Gharāchyā puḍhe wa māge āngaṇ āhe.

Angaṇāt bāg āhe.

Bāget phoolānchee zāde āhet.

Gharee waḍeel, āee, ek baheeṇa wa don bhāu āhet.

My House

This is my house.

There is a verandah in the house.

Boys are sitting on the verandah.

Beyond the verandah is the drawing-room.

There is a TV in the drawing-room.

There is a bedroom next to the drawing room.

There is a kitchen at the back.

At the other end of the house is a bath-room.

There is a courtyard in front and at the back of the house.

There is a garden in the courtyard.

There are flower trees in the garden.

Father, mother, a sister and two brothers are in the house.

—: o :—

LESSON 4

रस्ता

ह्या आमच्या शहरातील मुख्य रस्ता आहे.

रस्त्याच्या दोन्ही बाजुना दुकाने आहेत.

दुकानात हरतऱ्हेचा माल भरलेला आहे.

विक्रेते गिऱ्हाइकांना माल दाखवीत आहेत.

दुपारी जेंव्हा दुकाने बंद होतात, तेंव्हा रस्त्यावरची रहदारी जरा कमी होते.

संध्याकाळी रस्ता वाहनांनी व लोकांनी भरुन जातो.

रस्त्याच्या अेका टोकाला मंदीर असून, दुसऱ्या टोकाला गुरुद्वारा आहे.

भक्तांची दोन्ही ठिकाणी नेहमी गर्दी असते.

—: o :—

Rastā

Ha āmachyā shaharāteel mukhya rastā āhe.

Rastyāchyā donhee bajunā dukāne āhet.

Dukānāt hartarhechā māl bharalelā āhe.

Vikrete girhaeekana māl dākhaveet āhet.

Dupāree jenhvā dukāne band hotāt, tenhvā rastyāvarchee rahadāree jarā kamee hote,

Sandhyākālee rastā wāhanānee wa lokānee bharoon jāto

Rastyāchyā ekā tokālā mandeer asoon, dusryā tokālā gurudwārā āhe.

Bhaktānchee donhee ṭhikāṇee nehmee gardee asate.

The Street

This is the main street of our city.

There are shops on both sides of the street.

The shops are full of various kinds of goods.

The salesmen are showing the customers the goods.

In the afternoon when the shops close, the traffic on the street lessens a little.

In the evening, the street gets filled with vehicles and people.

At one end of the street is a temple, while there is a gurudwara at the other end.

There is always a crowd of devotees at both the places.

—: o :—

LESSON 5

विद्यालय

ही विद्यालयाची इमारत आहे.

इमारतीत वर्गाच्या खोल्या आहेत.

वर्गात बाके व टेबले आहेत.

बाकावर विद्यार्थी बसले आहेत.

शिक्षक विद्यार्थ्यांना शिकवीत आहेत.

मुले पुस्तके वाचीत आहेत.

विद्यालयाची सुरुवात प्रार्थनेने होते.

इमारतीसमोर मैदान आहे.

मैदानात मुले व्यायाम करीत आहेत.

कांही मुले गात आहेत.

आता विद्यालयाची मधली सुट्टी झाली आहे.

—: o :—

Vidyālay

Hee Vidyālayāchee imārat āhe.

Imārateet vargāchyā kholyā āhet.

Vargāt bāke wa teble āhet.

Bākāwar vidyārthee basale āhet.

Shikshak vidyārthyānā shikaweet āhet.

Mule pustake wācheet āhet.

Vidyālayāchee suruwāt prārthanene hote.

Imārateesamor maidān āhe.

Maidānāt mule vyāyām kareet āhet.

Kāhee mule gāt āhet.

Atā vidyālayāchee madhalee suṭṭee zālee āhe.

The School

This is a school building.

In the building are classrooms.

There are benches and tables in the classrooms.

Pupils are seated on benches.

Teachers are teaching the pupils.

Boys are reading books.

The school starts with a prayer.

There is an open ground in front of the building.

In the ground boys are taking exercise.

Some boys are singing.

The school has now the lunch-break.

—: o :—

LESSON 6

मुंबई

महाराष्ट्र राज्याची राजधानी मुंबई हे भारतातील एक प्रमुख शहर व बंदर आहे.

मुंबई मुख्यत: ब्रिटीशांनी वसविली.

तसे पाहिले तर, मुंबई हे भारताच्या पश्चिम किनाऱ्याला लागून असलेले एक बेट आहे.

मुंबई हे अनेक उद्योगधंद्यांचे एक केन्द्र आहे.

भारतातील सर्व जातीजमातींचे लोक ह्या महानगरात राहतात.

हे शहर भारतातील प्रत्येक भागांशी रेलवे व विमान मार्गाने जोडले आहे.

खाडी पलिकडील भू-भागांवर नवीन मुंबई वसविण्याची योजना आता हाती घेण्यांत आली आहे.

—: o :—

Mumbaee

Mahārāshṭra rajyāchee rajdhānee mumbaee he bhāratāteel ek pramukh shahar wa bandar āhe.

Mumbaee mukhyatahā britishānee wasawilee.

Tase pāhile tar, mumbaee he bhāratāchyā pashcheem kināryālā lāgoon asalele ek beṭ āhe.

Mumbaee he anek udyogdhandyānche ek kendra āhe.

Bhāratāteel sarva jatee jamāteenche lok hyā shaharāt rāhatāt.

He shahar bhāratāteel pratyek bhāgāshee relwe wa vimān mārgāne joḍle āhe.

Khāḍee palikaḍeel bhoo-bhāgāwar naveen mumbaee wasaweeṇyāchee yojanā ātā hātee ghenyāt ālee āhe.

Bombay

Bombay, the capital of the state of Maharashtra, is a leading city and port of India.

Bombay was mainly established by the British.

In fact, Bombay is an island off the west coast of India.

Bombay is the centre of several industries.

People of all the religions and castes of India live in this metropolis.

This city is linked with every part of India by railway and air.

The scheme of establishing New Bombay on the mainland across the creek has now been taken in hand.

—: o :—

LESSON 7

माझा व्यवसाय

Māzā Vyavasāy

My Profession

शाळेत जाणाऱ्या प्रत्येक विद्यार्थ्याला एखाद्या विशिष्ट व्यवसाया-बद्दल आकर्षण वाटत असते.

shālet jāṇaryā pratyek widyārthyālā ekhādyā wishishṭa vyavasāyābaddal ākarshaṇ wāṭaṭ asate.

Every schoolboy has an attraction for a particular profession.

कोणाला सैनिक व्हावेसे वाटते, कोणाला वैमानिक, तर कोणाला डॉक्टर अथवा वैज्ञानिक.

koṇālā sainik vhāwese wāṭate, koṇālā wai-mānik, tar koṇālā docṭar athawā wai-dnyānik !

One desires to become a soldier, another a pilot, while someone else wants to become a doctor or a scientist !

मी विद्यार्थी असताना माझा आवडता विषय मराठी होता.

mee widyārthee asatāna māzā āwaḍatā wishay marāṭhi hotā.

When I was a student, my favourite subject was Marathi.

आमचे मराठीचे शिक्षक मराठी फार चांगले शिकवीत.

āmache marāṭhiche shikshak marāṭhi phār chāngle shikaweet.

Our Marathi teacher taught Marathi very well.

त्यांच्या प्रमाणे मराठी भाषेत प्राविण्य मिळवावे अशी महत्वाकांक्षा माझ्या मनात निर्माण झाली.

tyānchyā pramāṇe marāṭhi bhāshet prāviṇya milawāwe ashee mahatwākānshā māzyā manāt nirmāṇ zalee.

An ambition to gain proficiency like his in the Marathi language was born in my mind.

मराठी साहित्याचा मी अभ्यास करु लागलो.

Marāṭhi sāhityāchā mee abhyās karu lāgalo.

I began to study Marathi literature.

एम.ए.ची परीक्षा पास झाल्यानंतर मला आमच्या शाळेत शिक्षकाची नोकरी मिळाली.

M.A.chee pareekshā pāṣ zālyānantar. malā āmchyā shāḷet shikshakāchee nokri miḷālee.

After passing the M.A. examination, I got a job in our school as a teacher.

मराठी भाषा शिकविण्यांत मला आनंद वाटतो.

Marāṭhi bhāshā shikaviṇyāt malā ānand wāṭato.

I enjoy teaching the Marathi language.

—: o :—

LESSON 8

नाती

Nāti

Relations

माझे वडील एका वर्तमानपत्राचे संपादक आहेत.

māze waḍeel eka wartamānpatrāche sampādak āhet.

My father is an editor of a newspaper.

आई गृहिणी आहे.

āee gruhiṇee āhe.

Mother is a housewife.

माझी बहीण एका कॉलेजात शिकते व भाऊ एका कारखान्यात एंजिनिअर म्हणून नोकरी करतो.

māzee baheeṇ ekā collejāt shikate wa bhāu ekā kārkhāṇyāt engineer mhaṇoon nokri karato.

My sister studies in a college and a brother works in a factory as an engineer.

आजोबा घरी रामायण वाचतात आणि आजी देवळात जाते.

ājobā gharee rāmāyaṇ wāchatāt āṇee ājee devalāt jāte.

Grandpa reads the Ramayan at home and grandma goes to a temple.

माझे काका व काकी शेतावर रहातात.

māze kākā wa kākee shetāwar rahātāt.

My uncle and aunt live on a farm.

माझे सासरे नागपुर हायकोर्टात वकीली करतात.

māze sāsare nāgpur highcourtat wakeelee kartāt.

My father-in-law practises law at the Nagpur High Court.

माझी सासु एका अनाथ बालकाश्रमाची संचालिका आहे.

māzee sāsu ekā anāth bālakāshramāchee sanchālikā āhe.

My mother-in-law is a superintendent of a home for destitute children.

माझे मेहुणे व मेहुणी बँकेत नोकरी करतात.

māze mehuṇe wa mehuṇee banket nokri karatāt.

My brother-in-law and sister-in-law work in a bank.

माझी पत्नी एका मुलींच्या शाळेत शिक्षिका आहे.

māzee patnee ekā mulinchyā shāḷet shikshikā āhe.

My wife is a teacher in a girl's school.

माझा मुलगा डॉक्टर आहे. तो पुणे शहरात प्रॅक्टीस करतो.

māzā mulagā docṭar āhe. To puṇe shaharāt practice karato.

My son is a doctor. He practises in the city of Pune.

माझ्या मुलीचे लग्न झाले असून माझे जावई दिल्लीस सरकारी नोकरीत असतात.

māzyā muleeche lagna zāle asoon māze jāwaee dillis sarakāri nokrit asatāt.

My daughter is married and my son-in-law is in Government service at Delhi.

—: o :—

LESSON 9

सहल
Sahal
Picnic

दैनंदिन तेच ते काम करीत असता आपण थकून जातो.

damandin tech te kām kareet asatā āpaṇa thakoon jāto.

By doing the same chores every day we get tired.

हा थकवा घालवून ताजेतवाने होण्याकरीता कधी कधी सहलीवर जाणे चांगले असते.

ha thakawā ghālawoon tājetawāne hoṇyā-kareetā kadhee kadhee sahaleewar jāṇe chāngale asate.

It is good to mitigate this weariness and refresh ourselves by going on a picnic sometimes.

काही दिवसापूर्वी मी मित्रांबरोबर फरीदाबाद नजीक बदकल तलावावर सहलीला गेलो होतो.

kāhec diwasāpurvee mee mitranbarobar Faridābād ṇajeek Badkal talāwāwar sahaleelā gelo hoto.

A few days ago I had gone with friends on a picnic to the Badkal lake near Faridabad.

आम्ही तेथे बसने सकाळी नऊ वाजता पोचलो.

āmhee tethe basne sakāḷee naoo wājatā pochalo.

We got there by bus at nine in the morning.

तलावाच्या किनाऱ्याला लागून एक सुंदर बाग आहे.

talāwāchyā kināryālā lāgoon ek sundar bāg āhe.

There is a beautiful garden along the bank of the lake.

तलावात नौकाविहार करता येतो.

talāwāt naukawihār karatā yeto.

One can go boating in the lake.

आम्ही नौकेतून तलावाची एक फेरी मारली.

āmhee nauketoon talāwāchee ek pheree māralee.

We made a round of the lake in a boat.

दुपारच्या जेवणानंतर आम्ही सर्वांनी काही वेळ विश्रांती घेतली.

dupārchyā jewaṇānantar āmhee sarwānee kāhee weḷ wishrāntee ghetlee.

After the midday meal all of us rested for a while.

संध्याकाळी आम्ही बागेत फेरफटका मारला.

sandhyākāḷee āmhee bāget pherphaṭakā mārlā.

In the evening we roamed about in the garden.

अशा तर्‌हेने मी मित्रांच्या सहवासात दिवस मजेत घालविला.

ashā tarhene mee mitrānchyā sahawāsāt diwas majet ghālawilā.

Thus, I spent a pleasant day in the company of friehds.

—: o :—

LESSON 10

लग्न-समारंभ
Lagna-samārambha
A Wedding Ceremony

लग्न हा धार्मिक विधी सर्व समाजात असतो.

lagna hā dhārmik widhee sarva samājāt asato.

A wedding as a religious rite is present in all societies.

ह्या समारभाद्वारे पुरुष व स्त्री पती-पत्नीच्या मंगल बंधनाने कायमचे एकत्र येतात.

hyā samārambhādwāre purush wa stree patee-patneechyā mangal bandhanāne kāyamche ekatra yetāt.

Through this ceremony, a man and a woman unite with each other externally in holy wedlock.

वराने व वधुने यज्ञाच्या पवित्र अग्नीला सात प्रदक्षिणा घातल्यानंतर, ते एकमेकांच्या गळयांत पुष्पमाला घालतात.

warāne wa wadhune yadnyāchyā pavitra agneelā sāt pradakshiṇā ghātlyānantar, te ekmekanchyā gaḷyāt pushpamālā ghāltāt.

After they have gone round the sacred fire of 'yadnya' seven times, the bride and the bridegroom place garlands around each other's necks.

त्या नंतर वधु-वरांची वरात निघते.

tyānantar wadhu-warānchee warāt nighate.

Thereafter the bride and the bridegroom are taken out in a procession.

शेवटी सर्व उपस्थित पाहुण्यांना मेजवानी दिली जाते.

shewaṭee sarva upasthit pahuṇyānā mejwānee dilee jāte.

At the end all the guests that are present are given a banquet.

—: o :—

LESSON 11

एक प्रवास
Ek Prawās
A Journey

शंकरने दिल्ली ते मुंबई हा प्रवास आगगाडीने केला.

Shankarne dilli te mumbaee hā prawās āga-gāḍeene kelā.

Shankar made the journey from Delhi to Bombay by railway.

वाटेत मथुरा, आग्रा, ग्वाल्हेर, नाशिक इत्यादि अनेक शहरे लागली.

wāṭet Mathura, Agra, Gwalior, Nashik ityādi anek shahare lāglee.

On the way he passed through many cities such as Mathura, Agra, Gwalior, Nashik and so on.

प्रत्येक स्टेशनवर प्रवाशांची गर्दी होत असे.

pratyek steshanwar prawāshānchee gardee hot ase.

At every station, there would be a crowd of passengers.

शंकरच्या डब्यात मात्र थोडेच लोक होते.

Shankarchyā ḍabyāt matra ṭhoḍech lok hote.

There were, however, only a few people in Shankar's compartment.

चोवीस तासांचा हा प्रवास शंकरला खूप आवडला.

chowees tāsanchā hā prawās Shankarlā khoop āwaḍlā.

Shankar liked this journey of twenty-four hours very much.

—: o :—

LESSON 12

महाराष्ट्र
Mahārāshṭra

भारताच्या संघराज्यापैकी महाराष्ट्र हे एक राज्य आहे.

Bharatāchyā sangharājyāpaikee mahārāshṭra he ek rājyā āhe.

Maharashtra is one of India's federal states.

ह्या राज्याची सीमा पश्चिमेकडे अरबी समुद्रापासून पूर्वेकडे नागपूर पलीकडे असलेल्या भंडारा शहरापर्यंत पसरली आहे.

hyā rājyāchee seemā paschimekaḍe arabee samudrāpāsoon purvekaḍe nāgpur paleekaḍe asalelyā bhandārā shaharāparyant pasaralee āhe.

The border of this state extends from the Arabian Sea on the west eastwards to the city of Bhandara beyond Nagpur.

सह्याद्रि पर्वताने महाराष्ट्राची देश व कोकण अशा दोन भागात विभागणी केली आहे.

sahyādri parvatāne mahārāshṭrāchee desh wa kokan ashā don bhāgāt wibhāgaṇee kelee āhe.

The Sahyadri mountain has divided Maharashtra into the two regions of Desh and Konkan.

गोदावरी, कृष्णा, भिमा व वर्धा ह्या महाराष्ट्राच्या प्रमुख नद्या आहेत.

godāvaree, krishṇā, bhimā wa wardhā hyā mahārāshṭrāchyā pramukh nadyā āhet.

Godavari, Krishna, Bhima and Wardha are the principal rivers of Maharashtra.

कोकण, पश्चिम महाराष्ट्र, मराठवाडा व विदर्भ अशा चार विभागामिळुन महाराष्ट्र बनला आहे.

kokan, pashchim mahārāshṭra, marāthwāḍā wa widarbha ashā chār wibhāgāmiloon mahārāshṭra banalā āhe.

Maharashtra is made up of the four regions of Konkan, Western Maharashtra, Marathwada and Vidarbha.

काजू, नारळ, आंबे, व तांदुळ ही कोकणपट्टीची मुख्य पिके असून, अन्यत्र मुख्यतः गहु, तांदुळ, ऊस व कापूस पिकतो.

kājoo, nāraḷ, āmba wa tāndul hee kokanpaṭṭeechee mukhya pike asoon, anyatra mukhyatahā gahu, tānḍuḷ, oos wa kāpoos pikato.

Cashew, coconut, mango and rice are the principal crops of the Konkan strip, while elsewhere wheat, rice, sugarcane and cotton are mostly grown.

रत्नागिरी हे कोकणातील, मुबई, पुणे व नाशिक ही पश्चिम महाराष्ट्रातील, औरंगाबाद व नाँदेड ही मराठवाडयातील, आणि नागपूर, अकोला व चंद्रपूर ही विदर्भातील मोठी शहरे आहेत.

Ratnāgiri he kokaṇāteel, mumbaee, puṇe, wa nashik hee pashchim mahārāshṭrāteel, aurangābād wa nānded hee marāthwāḍyāteel āṇee nāgpur, akolā wa chandrapur hee widarbhāteel moṭhee shahare āhet.

Ratnagiri in the Konkan, Bombay, Puṇe and Nasik in Western Maharashtra, Aurangabad and Nanded in Marathwada and Nagpur, Akola, and Chandrapur in Vidarbha are the large cities.

महाराष्ट्राची लोकसख्या पाच कोटींच्या वर असून क्षत्रफळ सुमारे तीन लाख वर्ग किलोमीटर आहे.

mahārāshṭrāchee lokasankhyā pach koṭeenchyā war asoon kshetraphal sumāre teen lakh warga kilomiṭar āhe.

The population of Maharashtra exceeds five crores, while its land area measures approximately three lakh square kilometres.

शिवाजी, बाळ गंगाधर टिळक, सावरकर व आंबेडकर ह्या थोर भारतीयांना महाराष्ट्राने जन्म दिला.

Shivājee, baḷ gangādhar tiḷak, sāwarkar wa āmbeḍkar hya thor bhāratiyānā mahārāshṭrāne janma dila.

Shivaji, Bal Gangadhar Tilak, Sawarkar and Ambedkar are the great Indians Maharashtra has given birth to.

—: o :—

LESSON 13

खरेदी
Kharedee
Shopping

वीणाला तीच्या मुलांसाठी कपडे खरेदी करायचे आहेत.

Veeṇālā teechyā mulansāṭhee kapaḍe kharedee karāyache āhet.

Veena wants to buy clothes for her children.

म्हणुन ती एका कपड्यांचा दुकानात जाते.

mhaṇoon tee ekā kapaḍyānchyā dukānāt jāte.

Hence she goes to a garment store.

दुकानात प्रवेश केल्यानंतर ती एका विक्रेत्याकडे जाते.

dukānāt pravesh kelyānantar tee ekā vikretyākaḍe jāte.

After entering the store, she goes to a salesman.

वीणा : आपल्याकडे लहान मुलांसाठी तयार कपडे आहेत काय ?

Veeṇā· āpalyākaḍe lahān mulansāṭhee tayār kapaḍe āhet kāy ?

Veena: Do you have readymade clothes for children ?

विक्रेता: हो आहेत. आपणास किती वर्षे वयाच्या मुलांसांठी कपडे हवेत ?

Vikretā· ho āhet. Apaṇās kitee varshe vayāchyā mulansāṭhee kapaḍe havet ?

Salesman: Yes, we have. For children of what age do you want clothes ?

वीणा : मला आठ वर्षाच्या मुलासाठी एक टी-शर्ट व अकरा वर्षाच्या मुलीसाठी एक फ्रॉक हवा आहे.

Veeṇā: malā āṭh varshāchyā mulāsāṭhee ek T-shirṭ wa akarā varshāchyā muleesāṭhee ek frock hawā āhe.

Veena: I want a T-shirt for an eight-year-old boy and a frock for an eleven-year-old girl.

विक्रेता: ह्या वयाच्या मुलामुलींसाठी आमच्याकडे अनेक प्रकारचे तयार कपडे आहेत. त्या काउंटरवर या. मी आपणास ते दाखवितो.

Vikretā : hyā vayāchyā mulāmuleensāṭhee āmachyākaḍe anek prakārche tayār kapaḍe āhet. tyā counṭervar yā. Mee āpaṇās te dākhavito.

Salesman: We have several kinds of readymade clothes for boys and girls of these ages. Come to that counter. I shall show them to you.

वीणा : हा फ्रॉक छान आहे. कॉटनचा आहे की टेरीकॉटचा ?

Veeṇā: hā frock chhān āhe. Coṭṭanchā āhe kee ṭerricoṭchā ?

Veena: This is a nice frock. Is it of cotton or teryicot ?

विक्रेता: हा फ्रॉक उत्तम प्रतीच्या कापसापासून बनविला आहे.

Vikretā· hā frock ut tam pratichyā kāpasāpasoon banavilā āhe.

Salesman: This frock is made of best quality cotton.

वीणा : किंमत किती ?

Veeṇā: kimmat kitee ?

Veena: How much is it ?

विक्रेता: ह्या फ्रॉकची किंमत पन्नास रुपये आहे.

Vikretā: hyā frockchee kimmat pannas rupee āhe

Salesman: The price of this frock is rupees fifty.

वीणा : ठीक आहे, मी तो घेते. आता एखादा चांगलासा टी-शर्ट दाखवा.

Veeṇā ṭheek āhe, mee to ghete. ātā ekhādā chāngalāsā T-shirt dākhwā.

Veena: OK, I shall take it. Now, show me a nice T-shirt.

विक्रेता: हा टी-शर्ट कसा वाटतो तुम्हाला ? किमत ही फार नाही. फक्त बत्तीस रुपये.

Vikretā: hā T-shirt kasā wāṭato tumhālā ? kimmat hee phār nāhee. fakta battees rupaye.

Salesman: What do you think of this T-shirt ? It is also not very expensive. Only thirty-two rupees.

वीणा : किमत वाजवी आहे, पण आटणार नाही ना तो ?

Veeṇā: kimmat wājawee āhe, paṇ ātaṇār nāhee nā to ?

Veena: The price is reasonable, but won't it shrink ?

विक्रेता: नाही बाईसाहेब. त्या बद्दल खात्री असु द्या. आटल्यास आम्ही शर्ट परत घेऊ.

Vikretā: nāhee bāeesāheb. tyā bad-dal khātree asoo dyā. āṭalyās āmhee shirṭ parat ghe-oo.

Salesman: No madam. Rest assured about that. If it shrinks, we shall take it back.

वीणा : बरे आहे, दोन्ही कपडे बांधुन द्या.

Veeṇā: bare āhe, donhee kapaḍe bāndhun dyā.

Veena: Very well, pack the two garments.

—: o :—

LESSON 14

म्हणी
Mhaṇee
Proverbs

1 करावे तसे भरावे.

Karāve tase bharāve.

As you sow, so you reap.

2 गर्जेल तो पडेल काय ?

Garjel to paḍel kay ?

Barking dogs seldom bite.

3 नाचता येईना, आंगण वाकडे.

Nāchatā ye-eenā, āngaṇ wākaḍe.

A bad workman quarrels with his tools

4 एका माळेचे मणी.

Ekā māḷeche manee.

Birds of the same feather.

5 अंथरुण पाहून पाय पसरावे.

Antharooṇ pāhoon pāy pasarāwe.

Cut your coat according to the cloth.

6 मुलाचे पाय पाळण्यांत दिसतात.

Mulāche pāy pāḷaṇyāt distāt

Coming events cast their shadows before them.

7 दुरुन डोंगर साजरे.

Duroon ḍongar sājare.

Distance lends enchantment to the view.

8 उथळ पाण्याला खळखळाट फार.

Uthaḷ pāṇyālā khaḷkhaḷāṭ phār.

Empty vessels make most noise.

9 चार दिवस सासूचे, चार दिवस सुनेचे.

Chār divas sāsooche, chār divas suneche.

Every dog has his day.

10 भिंतीला कान असतात.

Bhinteelā kān asatāt.

Walls have ears.

11 एका हाताने टाळी वाजत नाही.

Ekā hātāne ṭāḷee wājat nāhee.

It takes two to make a quarrel.

12 दिव्या खाली अंधार.

Divyā khālee andhār.

It is dark under the lamp.

13 बाप तसा बेटा.

Bāp tasā beṭa.

Like father, like son.

14 डोंगर पोखरून उंदिर काढला.

Dongar pokharoon undir kāḍhalā.

A mountain in labour produces a mouse.

15 पैशाकडे पैसा जातो.

Paishākaḍe paisā jāto.

Money attracts money.

16 पिकते तेथे विकत नाही.

Pikate tethe vikat nāhee.

A prophet is not honoured in his own country.

17 चूक करणे हा मनुष्य स्वभाव आहे.

Chook karaṇe hā manushya swabhāv āhe.

To err is human.

18 देश तसा वेश.

Desh tasā vesh.

When in Rome, do as the Romans do.

—: o :—

GLOSSARY

Key : m = masculine noun
f = feminine noun
n = neuter noun
adj = adjective
v = verb

कारण (n) kāran	reason, because
कधी kadhee	when
केंव्हा kenvhā	when
कदाचित kadāchit	perhaps
करणे (v) karane	to do, to make
कसा kasā	how
कान (m) kān	ear
काय kāy	what
काही kāhee	some, a few
काल kāl	yesterday

कागद (m) kāgad	paper
कांदा (m) kāndā	onion
काम (n) kām	work, job
किती kitee	how many, how much
किंवा kinwā	or
किंमत (f) kimmat	price, cost
किल्ली (f) killee	key
कीव (f) keev	pity
कुत्रा (m) kutrā	dog
कुठे kuṭhe	where, where to
कुटुंब (n) kuṭumb	family
कुठून kuṭhoon	from where, whence
कुलुप (n) kulup	lock
केस (m) kes	hair
कैदी (m) kaidee	prisoner
कोण koṇ	who
कोणता (adj) koṇatā	which
कौतुक (n) kautuk	admiration, praise
कंदिल (m) kandil	lantern

खजिना (m) khajinā	treasure
खडा (m) khaḍā	a small stone
खडू (m) khaḍoo	chalk
खड्डा (m) khaḍ-da	pit
खाणे (v) khaṇe	to eat
खीर (f) kheer	a sweet porridge
खेळणे (v) khelane	to play
खेडे (n) kheḍe	village
खोली (f) kholee	room
खांब (m) khāmb	pillar
गवत (n) gawat	grass
गादी (f) gadee	mattress
गाय (f) gāy	cow
गाणे (v) gāṇe	to sing
गुण (m) guṇ	merit
गोदी (f) godee	docks
गोरा (adj) gorā	white, frir
*गंभीर (adj) gambheer	serious
घडी (f) ghəḍee	fold

घडी करणे (v) ghaḍee karaṇe	to fold
घालणे (v) ghālane	to insert
घाबरणे (v) ghābaraṇe	to get scared
घाम (m) ghām	sweat
घोडा (m) ghoḍā	horse
घूबड (n) ghubaḍ	owl
घेणे (v) gheṇe	to take
घेरी (f) gheree	faint
चव (f) chav	taste
चादर (f) chādar	a bedsheet
चिडणे (v) chiḍaṇe	to get angry
चुक (f) chuk	mistake, error
चुकणे (v) chukaṇe	to miss, to err
चेला (m) chelā	disciple, follower
चैन (f) chain	fun
चोर (m) chor	thief
चोरणे (v) choraṇe	to steal
छळणे (v) chhalaṇe	to torture

छत (n) chhat	roof
*छान (adj) chhān	nice
जग (n) jag	world
जागणे (v) jāgaṇe	to stay awake
जिंकणे (v) jinkaṇe	to win, to conquer
जुलुम (m) julum	oppression
जेंव्हा jenhvā	at that time (when)
जोर (m) jor	force
झबले (n) zabale	a child's frock
झाड (n) zāḍ	tree
झोपणे (v) zopaṇe	to sleep
झोप (f) zop	sleep
झोका (n) zokā	a swing
झेलणे (v) zelaṇe	to catch
झुंज (f) zunj	a fight
टक्कर (f) ṭakkar	a collision
टाकणे (v) ṭākaṇe	to leave, to throw
टाळणे (v) ṭāḷaṇe	to avoid

टिकणे (v) ṭikaṇe	to last, to endure
टोला (m) ṭolā	a blow
टोक (n) tok	tip, end
ठरविणे (v) ṭharaviṇe	to decide, to determine
ठाम ṭhām	firm, resolute
ठार मारणे ṭhār māraṇe	to kill
ठिणगी (f) ṭhiṇagee	spark
डबा (n) ḍabā	a box
डास (m) ḍās	a mosquito
डाग (m) ḍāg	a stain
ढग (m) ḍhag	a cloud
ढकलणे (v) ḍhekalaṇe	to push
ढाल (f) ḍhal	a shield
तवा (m) tawā	a frying-pan
ताप (m) tāp	fever
तापणे (v) tāpaṇe	to get hot
तार (f) tār	a wire
तीर (m) teer	an arrow; bank of river

तेल (n) tel	oil
तुप (n) tup	clarified butter (ghee)
तुसडा (adj) tusaḍā	rude
तुटणे (v) tuṭaṇe	to break, to snap
थकणे (v) thakaṇe	to get tired
थांबणे (v) thāmbaṇe	to wait
थुकणे (v) thunkaṇe	to spit
थोडा (adj) thoḍā	a little
दगड (m) dagaḍ	a stone
दरवाजा (m) darawājā	a door
दाखविणे (v) dākhaviṇe	to show, to point out
दिशा (f) dishā	direction
दिवा (m) divā	a lamp
दिवस (m) divas	a day
दिवसा divasā	during day time
दुकान (n) dukān	a shop
दूर door	far away, distant
देणे (v) deṇe	to give
दिसणे (v) disaṇe	to see, to come into view

दोर (m) dor	a rope
देश (m) desh	a country
दुध (n) dudh	milk
धरणे (v) dharaṇe	to catch hold of
धावणे (v) dhāvaṇe	to run
धातु (m) dhātu	an alloy, a metal
धूर (m) dhoor	smoke
धूसर dhoosar	smoky, unclear
धुणे dhuṇe	to wash
धोका (m) dhokā	danger
धंदा (m) dhandā	trade, profession, calling
नकार (m) nakār	refusal
नाक (n) nāk	nose
नासणे (v) nāsane	to get spoiled
नाही nāhee	no, not
निघणे (v) nighaṇe	to start
नेणे (v) neṇe	to take away, to carry away
नेमणे (v) nemaṇe	to appoint

नेसणे (v) nesaṇe	to wear
निसर्ग (m) nisarga	nature
पडणे (v) paḍaṇe	to fall
पाऊस (m) pāoos	rain
पाऊस पडणे pāoos paḍaṇe	to rain
पाडणे (v) pāḍaṇe	to cause to fall
पान (f) pān	a leaf
पिणे (v) piṇe	to drink
पुरुष (m) purush	a man
पोट (n) poṭa	stomach
पोपट (m) popaṭ	a parrot
पळणे (v) paḷaṇe	to run
पैसा (m) paisā	money
पंडित (m) panḍit	a learned man
फसणे (v) fasaṇe	to get deceived
फसविणे (v) fasaviṇe	to deceive
फांदी (f) fandee	branch of a tree
फिरणे (v) firaṇe	to stroll,toramble

फिरविणे (v) firaviṇe	to turn
फुल (n) ful	a flower
फेकणे (v) fekaṇe	to throw
फुगा (m) foogā	a balloon
फार fār	much
बदक (n) badak	a duck
बहिरा (adj) bahirā	deaf
बाहेर bāher	outside
बाग (f) bāg	a garden
बांगडी (f) bāngaḍee	a bangle
बासरी (f) bāsaree	a flute
*बारीक (adj) bāreek	thin
बुडणे (v) buḍaṇe	to get drowned
बोलणे (v) bolaṇe	to speak, to talk
बैल (m) baeel	a bullock, an ox
भक्त (m) bhakta	a devotee
भरणे (v) bharaṇe	to fill
भार (m) bhār	load, weight

भिजणे (v) bhijaṇe	to get wet
भिणे (v) bhiṇe	to get frightened
भिंत (f) bhint	a wall
भूत (n) bhoot	a ghost
भूक (f) bhook	hunger
भेटणे bheṭaṇe	to meet
भेट (f) bheṭ	a meeting
भोक (n) bhok	a hole, an orifice
भिकारी (m) bhikāree	a beggar
*मऊ (adj) maoo	soft
मागणे (v) māgaṇe	to ask for, to supplicate
मारणे (v) māraṇe	to beat, to kill
ममता (f) mamatā	affection
मिसळणे (v) misaḷaṇe	to mix
मिळणे (v) milane	to get
*मुर्ख (adj) murkha	stupid, foolish
मुलगा (m) mulagā	a boy, a lad
मुलगी (f) mulagee	a girl, a lass
मुल (n) mool	a child, a baby

मुले (plural) mule	children
मोजणे (v) mojaṇe	to measure. to count
मेव्हणा (m) mevhaṇa	brother-in-law
मेव्हणी (f) mevhaṇee	sister-in-law
मित्र (m) mitra	friend
मैत्रिण (f) maitreeṇ	girl-friend
मैत्री (f) maitree	friendship
यंत्र (n) yantra	machine, instrument
यातना (f) yātanā	torture
याचना (f) yāchanā	request, supplication
यात्रा (f) yātrā	pilgrimage
युवक (m) yuwak	a young man
युवती (f) yuwati	a young woman
यौवन (n) youwan	youth
येणे (v) yene	to come
*योग्य (adj) yogya	proper, suitable
योजना (f) yojanā	programme, plan
योजणे (v) yojane	to plan

रक्त (n) rakta	blood
रस (m) ras	juice
रमणे (v) ramaṇe	to get engrossed in
राग (m) rāg	anger
रजइ (f) rajai	blanket
रागावणे (v) rāgāvaṇe	to scold, to chide
रडणे (v) radaṇe	to cry, to weep
*रेशमी (adj) reshamee	silken
रुमाल (m) rumāl	handkerchief
रोग (m) rog	disease, ailment

*लबाड (adj) labāḍ	dishonest
लवकर lawakar	soon, quickly
लसूण (m) lasooṇ	garlic
*लहान (adj) lahān	small, young
लाज (f) lāj	shame
लिहिणे (v) lihiṇe	to write
लेख (m) lekh	a written article, an essay
लेखक (m) lekhak	a writer, an author

लेखिका (f) lekhikā	a woman writer, authoress
लोक (plural) lok	people
लोकर (f) lokar	wool
लुबाडणे (v) lubāḍaṇe	to rob
वजन (n) vajan	weight
वागणे (v) vāgaṇe	to behave
वागणूक (n) vāg nook	behaviour
विसरणे (v) visaraṇe	to forget
विष (n) vish	poison
वेगळा (adj) vegaḷa	different
वाघ (m) vāgh	a tiger
वाघिण (f) vāghiṇa	a tigress
शब्द (m) shabda	a word
शपथ (f) shapath	an oath
शपथ घेणे (v) shapath gheṇe	to take an oath
शाल (f) shāl	shawl
*शांत (adj) shānt	quiet
शांतता (f) shāntatā	peace, quiet

शंका (f) shankā	doubt
शस्त्र (n) shastra	weapon
*शुद्ध (adj) shuddha	pure
शिकणे (v) shikaṇe	to learn
शिकविणे (v) shikaviṇe	to teach
शिकार करणे (v) shikār karaṇe	to hunt
शोध (m) shodh	search, quest
*शूर (adj) shoor	brave, valiant
शौर्य (n) shourya	bravery, courage
सत्य (n) satya	truth
सांगणे (v) sāngaṇe	to tell
संपणे (v) sampaṇe	to come to an end, to exhaust
सा (m) sāp	a snake
संगीत (n) sangit	music
सूर (m) soor	a tune
सैन्य (n) sainya	an army
समुद्र (m) samudra	an ocean
सहानुभूति(f) sahānubhooti	sympathy

सुगंध (m) sugandha	fragrance
*सैल (adj) sail	loose
सोपा (adj) sopā	easy, simple
सासु (f) sāsu	mother-in-law
सासरा (m) sāsarā	father-in-law
सून (f) soon	daughter-in-law
सुंदर (adj) sundar	beautiful
संकट (n) sankaṭ	danger
सामान (n) sāmān	(household) articles, luggage
साधा (adj) sādhā	simple, easy
साधन (n) sādhan	means
हक्क (m) hak-ka	right, privilege
हरविणे (v) haraviṇe	to lose, to defeat
हरणे (v) haraṇe	to be defeated
होकार (m) hokār	consent
क्षमा (f) kshamā	pardon
क्षमा करणे (v) kshamā karaṇe	to pardon, to forgive

*अमर (adj) amar	immortal
अंतर (n) antar	distance
आत āt	in, inside
आत येणें (v) āt yeṇe	to enter, to come in
आग (f) āg	fire
आंबा (m) āmbā	mango
अंधार (m) andhār	darkness
अंधार पडणे (v) andhār paḍaṇe	to get dark
आशा (f) āshā	hope
इतर itar	other
इमारत (f) imārat	a building
उंदिर (m) oondir	a rat
उंट (m) oonta	a camel
उगाच ugāch	in vain
*उदास (adj) udās	melancholy, dejected
उत्तर (n) uttar	answer
उशी (f) ushee	pillow
अेकटा (m) ekata	alone (mas)
अेकटी (f) ekatee	alone (fem)

अैट (f) aet	pomp, show
ओरडणे (v) oraḍaṇe	to shout
ओकणे (v) okane	to vomit
इच्छा (f) ich-chhā	wish, desire
इच्छा करणे (v) ich-chhā karaṇe	to wish, to desire
ईश्वर (m) ishwar	God

*has only one adjectival form, common to mas., fem., neu.

—: o :—

1
2
3
4
5
6
7
8
9
10
11
12
13
14
15
16
17
18
19
SOAP

Around the House

1.	Pillow	उशी	ushee (f)
2.	Bedsheet	चादर	chādar (f)
3.	Blanket	रजइ	rajai (f)
4.	Mattress	गादी	gādee (f)
5.	Bed	पलंग	palang (m)
6.	Door	दरवाजा	darawājā (m)
7.	Basket	परडी	paraḍee (f)
8.	Rug	रजइ	rajai (f)
9.	Telephone	टेलिफोन	teliphon (m)
10.	Picture	चित्र	chitra (n)
11.	Flower vase	फुलदाणी	fuladāṇee (f)
12.	Tablecloth	टेबलक्लॉथ	tebalcloth (n)
13.	Mirror	आरसा	ārasā (m)
14.	Swing	झोका	zokā (m)
15.	Towel	पंचा	panchā (m)
16.	Letter	पत्र	patra (n)
17.	Shoe	जोडा	jodā (m)
18.	Stairs	जिना	jinā (m)
19.	Soap	साबु	sābu (m)

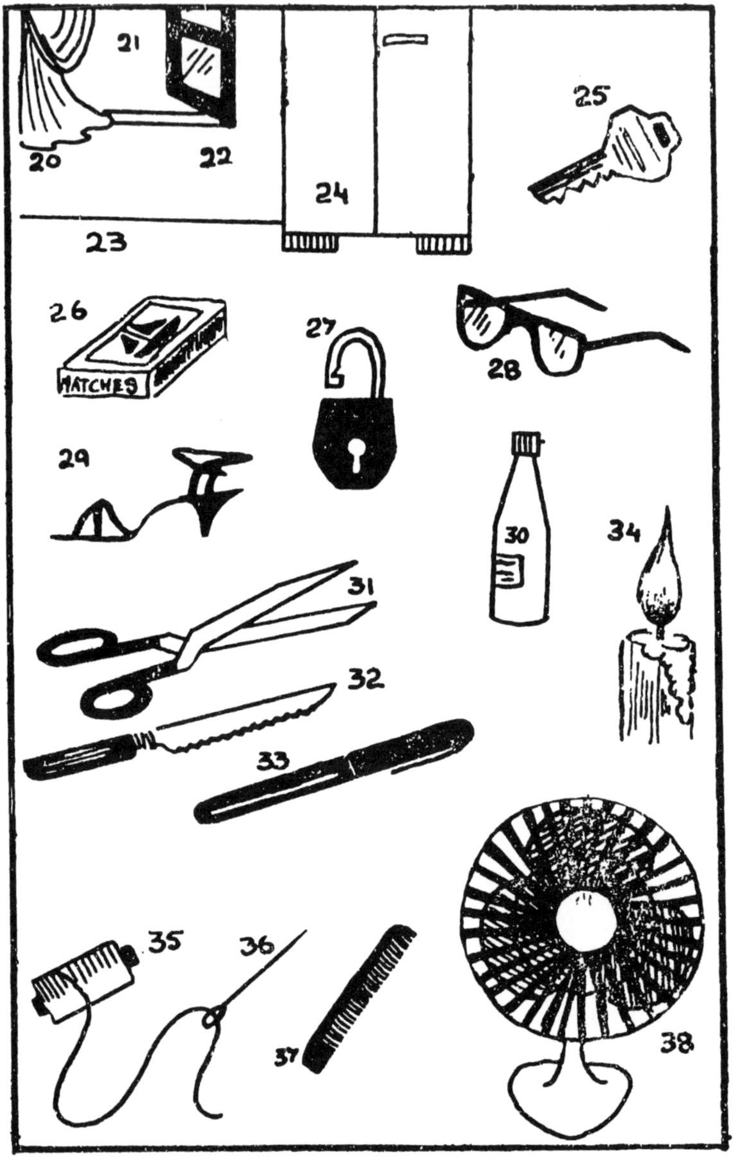

21
20
22
24
25
23
26
MATCHES
27
28
29
30
34
31
32
33
35
36
37
38

20. Curtain	पडदा	paḍadā (m)
21. Window	खिडकी	khidkee (f)
22. Wall	भिंत	bhint (f)
23. Floor	जमीन	jameen (f)
24. Almirah	कपाट	kapāt (n)
25. Key	किल्ली	kil-lee
26. Match	काडी	kādee (f)
27. Lock	कुलुप	kulup (n)
28. Spectacles	चष्मा	chashmā (m)
29. Sandal	चप्पल	chappal (f)
30. Bottle	बाटली	bātalee (f)
31. Scissors	कातर	kātar (f)
32. Knife	चाकु	chāku (m)
33. Pen	लेखणी	lekhaṇee (f)
34. Candle	मेणबत्ती	meṇabattee (f)
35. Thread	दोरा	dorā (m)
36. Needle	सुइ	su-ee (f)
37. Comb	कंगवा	kāngawā(m)
38. Fan	पंखा	pankhā (m)

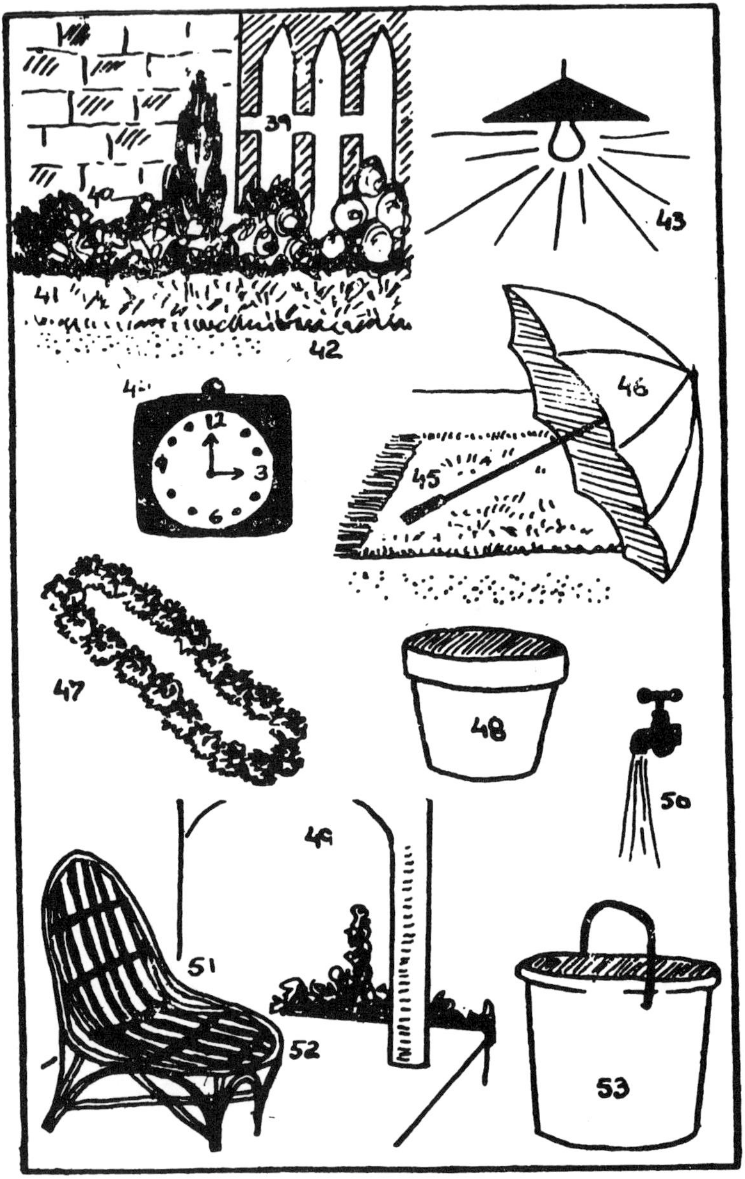
39
40
41
42
43
44
45
46
47
48
49
50
51
52
53

39.	Fence	कुंपण	kumpaṇa (n)
40.	Flower-bed	वाफा	wāfā (m)
41.	Grass	गवत	gawat (n)
42.	Road	रस्ता	rastā (m)
43.	Light	प्रकाश	prakāsh (m)
44.	Clock	घडयाळ	ghaḍyāḷa (n)
45.	Carpet	गालिचा	gālichā (m)
46.	Umbrella	छत्री	chhatree (f)
47.	Garland	हार	hār (m)
48.	Flower-pot	फुलदाणी	fuldāṇee (f)
49.	Verandah	ओसरी	osaree (f)
50.	Water	पाणी	pānee (n)
51.	Cane chair	वेताची खुर्ची	wetāchee khurchee
52.	Cane	वेत	wet
53.	Bucket	बादली	bādalee

Other Hippocrene Titles of Regional Interest

FLAVORFUL INDIA
2-Color • 180 pages • 6 x 9 • $22.50hc • 0-7818-1060-4 • (92)

THE INDIAN SPICE KITCHEN
240 pages • 8 x 10¼ • color photographs • $17.50pb • 0-7818-0801-4 • (513)

HEALTHY SOUTH INDIAN COOKING
348 pages • 5½ x 8½ • color photographs • $24.95hc • 0-7818-0867-7 • (69)

INDIA: AN ILLUSTRATED HISTORY
200 pages • 5 x 7 • 50 b/w photos/ illustration/ maps • 0-7818-0944-4 • $14.95pb • (424)

TREASURY OF INDIAN LOVE
128 pages • 5 x 7 • 0-7818-0670-4 • $11.95hc • (768)

HINDI-ENGLISH/ENGLISH-HINDI DICTIONARY & PHRASEBOOK
3,400 entries • 210 pages • 3¾ x 7½ • 0-7818-0983-5 • $11.95pb • (488)

HINDI-ENGLISH/ENGLISH-HINDI STANDARD DICTIONARY
30,000 entries • 760 pages • 5 x 8 • 0-7818-0470-1 • $27.50pb • (559)

HINDI-ENGLISH/ENGLISH-HINDI PRACTICAL DICTIONARY
25,000 entries • 399 pages • $4\frac{3}{8}$ x 7 • 0-7818-0084-6 • $19.95pb • (362)

TEACH YOURSELF HINDI
207 pages • 5½ x 8½ • 0-87052-831-9 • $8.95pb • (170)

PUNJABI-ENGLISH/ENGLISH-PUNJABI DICTIONARY
25,000 entries • 782 pages • 5 x 7½ • 0-7818-0940-1 • $19.95pb • (401)

SANSKRIT-ENGLISH CONCISE DICTIONARY
18,000 pages • 380 pages • 4 x 6 • 0-7818-0203-2 • $14.95pb • (605)

SANSKRIT GRAMMAR FOR BEGINNERS
324 pages • 5 1/2 x 8 1/2 • 0-7818-1075-2 • $17.95pb • (135)

TAMIL-ENGLISH/ENGLISH-TAMIL DICTIONARY & PHRASEBOOK
6,000 entries • 250 pages • 3¾ x 7½ • 0-7818-1016-7 • $12.95pb • (81)

All prices subject to change without prior notice. To purchase Hippocrene Books contact your local bookstore, call (718) 454-2366, visit www.hippocrenebooks.com, or write to: Hippocrene Books, 171 Madison Avenue, New York, NY 10016. Please enclose check or money order, adding $5.00 shipping (UPS) for the first book and $.50 for each additional book.